TACTICAL ANALYSIS AND SESSIONS FROM BORUSSIA DORTMUND'S 4-2-3-1

WRITTEN BY

ATHANASIOS TERZIS

PUBLISHED BY

JURGEN KLOPP'S DEFENDING TACTICS

TACTICAL ANALYSIS AND SESSIONS FROM BORUSSIA DORTMUND'S 4-2-3-1

First Published January 2015 by SoccerTutor.com

Info@soccertutor.com | www.SoccerTutor.com

UK: 0208 1234 007 | US: (305) 767 4443 | ROTW: +44 208 1234 007

ISBN: 978-1-910491-03-4

Author

Athanasios Terzis © 2015

Edited by

Alex Fitzgerald - SoccerTutor.com

Cover Design by

Alex Macrides, Think Out Of The Box Ltd.
Email: design@thinkootb.com Tel: +44 (0) 208 144 3550

Diagrams

Diagram designs by SoccerTutor.com. All the diagrams in this book have been created using SoccerTutor.com Tactics Manager Software available from www.SoccerTutor.com

MEET THE AUTHOR - ATHANASIOS TERZIS

- UEFA 'B' Coaching licence
- M.S.C. in coaching and conditioning

I played for several teams in the Greek professional leagues. At the age of 29 I stopped playing and focused on studying football coaching. I have been head coach of several semi-pro football teams in Greece and worked as a technical director in the Academies of DOXA Dramas (Greek football league, 2nd division).

I wrote and published two books "4-3-3 the application of the system" and "4-4-2 with diamond in midfield, the application of the system" in Greek language. I then decided to proceed in something more specific so coaches would have an idea of how top teams apply the same systems. I published three further books with SoccerTutor.com Ltd which have become extremely successful and sold thousands worldwide:

1. ***FC Barcelona: A Tactical Analysis***
2. ***Jose Mourinho's Real Madrid: A Tactical Analysis***
3. ***FC Barcelona Training Sessions - 160 Practices from 34 Tactical Situations***

Analysing games tactically is a great love and strength of mine. I think teams have success only when they prepare well tactically. I have watched Borussia Dortmund in many of their league and Champions league matches for the last few years and all of them during the 2013-2014 season. Over 1000 hours of research has enabled me to present a full tactical blueprint of Borussia Dortmund and supporting training sessions in this book and the Jurgen Klopp's Attacking Tactics book (other part of this book set).

Borussia Dortmund used a mixed way of defending. They either applied aggressive pressing high up or dropped into the middle third to wait for the opposition players to arrive. Klopp did not hesitate to use both ways of defending during a match, so there were periods of intense pressing and periods of sitting back to wait. When sitting back, the team stayed very compact, then applied pressure to players who received between the forwards and the midfielders and tried to block the through passes from the defenders to the forwards. These tactics favoured the quick counter attacking style of Borussia Dortmund and led to many scoring chances.

During the negative transition, Borussia Dortmund tried to regain possession as quickly as possible and as high up the pitch as possible. This was achieved by retaining balance near the sidelines or in the centre, as well as retaining a safety player at all times.

Athanasios Terzis

CONTENTS

HOW THE TACTICAL ANALYSIS WAS PRODUCED FOR THIS BOOK

Athanasios Terzis has a great skill of analysing games tactically and watched every Borussia Dortmund game in the 2013-14 season. This book is made up of over 1000 hours of extensive research and analysis of Jurgen Klopp's side.

The Steps of Research and Analysis

1. Terzis watched the games, observing Borussia Dortmund's patterns of play and making notes.
2. Once the same phase of play occurred a number of times (at least 10) the tactics would be decoded and more detailed notes were written down, often separated according to the phases of the game and the various different tactical situations.
3. The positioning of each player on the pitch is studied in great detail, including their body shape.
4. Each individual movement with or without the ball was also recorded in detail.
5. Once all conceivable phases of play had been studied and analysed, SoccerTutor.com's Tactics Manager Software was used to create all of the diagrams in this book.
6. Finally, the key aspects of Borussia Dortmund's tactics were assessed and are explained clearly with notes and detailed descriptions.

How the Tactical Analysis is Used to Create Full Training Sessions

1. Athanasios Terzis is a UEFA 'B' coach and has provided a full and extensive analysis of Jurgen Klopp's Borussia Dortmund team, as explained above.
2. This analysis has been divided into specific tactical situations and has been used to create **14 Full Sessions (53 practices)** including:
    - Preventing Through Balls
    - Defending the Forward Run of the Full Back on the Weak Side
    - Dealing With the Extensive Shift Of A Centre Back Towards the Sideline (Covering The Position)
    - Retaining Balance in Midfield
    - Retaining a Safety Player
3. Have you got the Attacking part of this Book Set?

    The full analysis and training sessions are included for the Attacking Phase and the Transition from Defence to Attack.

JURGEN KLOPP AND BORUSSIA DORTMUND

Borussia Dortmund appointed Jurgen Klopp as the club's manager in May 2008 after disappointedly finishing in 13th place in the 2007-08 Bundesliga season. Dortmund won their first title under Klopp's management when they won the Super Cup against champions Bayern Munich in 2008. During Klopp's first season (2008-09) Borussia Dortmund finished in 6th place in the Bundesliga and 5th place in the next season.

During the 2010-11 season, Klopp led Dortmund to their first league title since 2002. Klopp then led his team to the club's first ever double (league title and German cup) in the 2011-12 season. Dortmund managed to win this championship with 81 points which set a new Bundesliga record at the time.

In the 2012-13 season, Dortmund reached the Champions League final against Bayern Munich, but they were defeated with a late goal from Arjen Robben. In both 2013 and 2014, Dortmund finished in second place in the Bundesliga and won the Super Cup by beating Bayern Munich twice, 4-2 and 2-0 respectively.

Klopp has managed to bring Borussia Dortmund back to not only amongst the top clubs in Germany, but also as one of the most fascinating and successful clubs in Europe.

JURGEN KLOPP

Coaching Roles & Honours

- Mainz 05 Head Coach (2001-2008)
- Borussia Dortmund Head Coach (2008 - Present)
- Bundesliga: 2011, 2012
- DFB-Pokal (German Cup): 2012
- DFL-Supercup: 2013, 2014
- UEFA Champions League runner–up: 2013

Individual Awards

- German Football Manager of the Year: 2011, 2012
- FIFA World Coach of the Year runner up: 2013

BORUSSIA DORTMUND'S PLAYERS
(4-2-3-1 FORMATION)

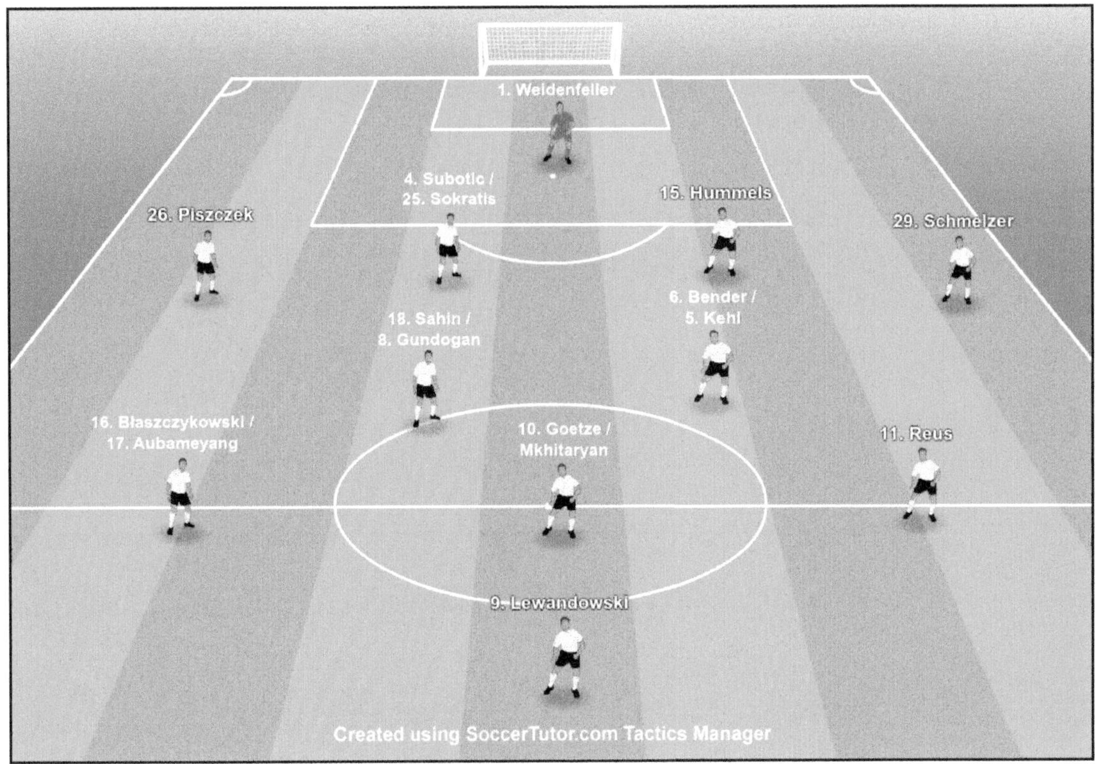

COACHING FORMAT

1. Tactical Situations and Analysis.
2. Full Session for the Tactical Situation.
   - Technical / Functional Unopposed Practices
   - Tactical Opposed Practices
   - Restrictions, Progressions, Variations & Coaching Points (if applicable)

KEY

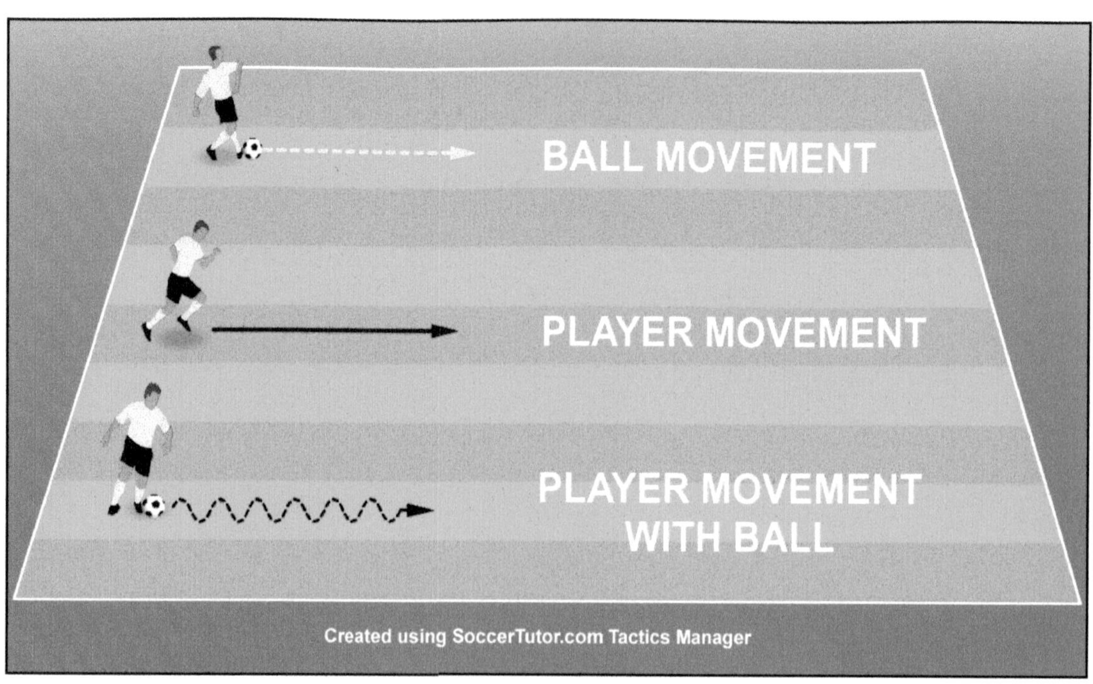

CHAPTER 1

BORUSSIA DORTMUND IN THE DEFENSIVE PHASE

The Defensive Phase

During the defensive phase, Borussia Dortmund mainly used two different tactics to deal with the opposition:

1. Borussia Dortmund usually pressed high up the pitch, even against the opposition goalkeeper or after the first pass towards one of the centre backs.
2. As an excellent counter attacking team there were periods during matches when the team dropped back into the middle third and waited for the opponents to come. This created space which Borussia Dortmund's players tried to take advantage of after winning possession.

Pressing

When pressing against various formations one of the main aims of the team was to reduce the available time and space for the player in possession. In order for this to take place, the players played at a high tempo, not only by moving quickly, but also by reading the tactical situations quickly.

Additionally Borussia Dortmund's players tried to force the ball towards the sidelines where the passing options for the player in possession were limited. So as soon as the ball was directed to an opponent near the sideline, pressure was immediately applied on him in order for the available time and space to be reduced.

Furthermore, all the players who were potential receivers were marked at close distance and in an ideal situation, superiority in numbers was created near the ball zone. If there was no possibility for all potential receivers to be marked, the less dangerous option (e.g. back pass) was left unmarked.

In the analysis to follow there will be a detailed analysis of the pressing application. We will present how the team dealt with teams that played with two defensive midfielders (such as 4-4-2 and 4-2-3-1) and one defensive midfielder (such as 4-3-3, 4-1-4-1 and 4-3-1-2).

Finally there will be also a presentation of how Borussia Dortmund dealt with teams that switched to a three man defence (3-4-3 formation).

CHAPTER 2

PRESSING AGAINST THE 4-4-2 / 4-2-3-1

Pressing Against Teams With Two Defensive Midfielders (4-4-2 / 4-2-3-1)

When playing against a team that used a solid 4-4-2 formation, there weren't any significant adaptations that the players had to make.

There was a perfect match up between the 4-2-3-1 and the 4-4-2 formation as the attacking midfielder Mkhitaryan used to play in a more advanced position as a second striker.

Starting Positions Against the 4-4-2 Formation

When the ball was in the goalkeeper's possession, the players took up the positions shown in the diagram. The centre forward and the central attacking midfielder (No.10) took up a more advanced position (compared to the other attacking midfielders) in order to be able to apply immediate pressure on the centre backs if the ball is directed to them. In addition, the No.10 usually positioned himself closer to the deeper placed (holding) defensive midfielder to control him.

Starting Positions Against the 4-2-3-1 Formation

Against the 4-2-3-1 formation the positioning was nearly the same, except the defensive midfielder (No.6) was closer to the opposition No.10.

Blocking The Passing Options For The Centre Back And Forcing The Ball Wide (Winger Is The First Defender)

When the first pass towards one of the centre backs was made, Borussia Dortmund's players had to prevent the dangerous passing options and force the ball towards the sideline. This pass was most often the pass towards the full back near the sideline.

Forcing the Ball Wide after the First Pass Towards the Centre Back (1)

The pressing was not always applied directly on the goalkeeper, but mainly started after the first pass towards one of the centre backs.

When the ball reached the centre back who was positioned towards the side where the No.10 was positioned, the aim of the players was to force the ball towards the sidelines (option 1) where the passing options were limited.

By blocking the vertical pass (option 2) towards the opposition winger (11), this enabled Borussia Dortmund's full back (26) to stay close to the other defenders and provide safety at the back rather than stepping up to close down his direct opponent which would create space for the opposing forwards.

By preventing the pass towards the inside (option 3), the team avoided a player receiving between the lines which would leave the two forwards (9 and 10) out of effective defensive positions and would give the man in possession the opportunity to have several passing options. In the situation above, the goalkeeper passes to red No.5 and Mkhitaryan (10) moves immediately to close the new man in possession down. Lewandowski (9) shifts towards the strong side, but remains in an advanced position in order to be ready to put pressure on the goalkeeper in case the ball is passed back to him.

Furthermore, this positioning is effective when Dortmund win possession and move into the positive transition phase (transition from defence to attack). In the above situation it is not essential for No.10 to block the back pass to the goalkeeper while applying pressure on the ball, because this kind of pass would be a risky choice for the reds due to the centre forward's advanced position. On the other hand the winger's (16) position enables him to block the potential vertical pass towards No.11. This makes it impossible for No.11 to receive and enables the full back (26) to stay together with the other defenders providing safety at the back.

Additionally, the defensive midfielder (18) has a double aim. He moves forward to mark No.6 who is a potential receiver and provides help to No.16 to narrow the vertical passing option at the same time. So the only available short passing option for No.5 is the one towards the full back No.3 (option 1).

Forcing the Ball Wide after the First Pass Towards the Centre Back (2)

In this similar situation to the previous one, Sahin (18) shifts to narrow the vertical passing lane.

As the opponent within his zone of responsibility (6) is away from being a potential receiver, Sahin can focus on narrowing the passing lane and providing support to Blaszczykowski (16). The vertical passing lane (option 2) is very narrow for a successful pass to be made and the only available option is the pass towards the left back No.3 near the sideline (option 1).

ASSESSMENT:

It must be mentioned that Sahin's (18) positioning is important in order to block the vertical pass and prevent the pass towards the inside. His positioning depends on the opposition defensive midfielder's (6) position.

If the opposition defensive midfielder is a potential receiver, Sahin (18) has to move into a more advanced position and mark him, whereas if he is away from receiving a potential pass, Sahin is mainly focused on blocking the vertical pass as well as providing support to the winger (16).

Tactical Analysis: Blocking Inside And Forward Passes

Situation 1 - Blocking the Inside Pass

The red centre back (5) receives the ball and all of Borussia Dortmund's players shift towards the strong side.

Sahin (18) not only shifts across to narrow the vertical passing lane, but also moves a few yards forward as the defensive midfielder (6) of the opposition moves towards the available passing lane.

No.5 passes inside to No.6 and Sahin (18) immediately applies pressure to prevent him from turning towards Dortmund's goal.

If the opposition player does manage to turn, the aim changes to try and force him to pass back or towards the sideline. No.9 and No.10 move close to the ball area, ready to intervene in case of a bad first touch or a successful intervention by Sahin. Bender (6) and Blaszczykowski (16) take up covering positions.

Situation 2 - Avoid Creating Space in Behind for the Opposition No.10

The red centre back (5) receives the ball and all of Borussia Dortmund's players shift towards the strong side. No.16 and No.18 move to prevent the vertical pass. As the red No.6 is unable to receive an inside pass, Sahin (18) is focused on blocking the vertical pass and providing support to No.16. The pass towards No.11 is difficult too, so the full back (26) does not move forward to mark him, but instead stays together with the other defenders to avoid creating space in behind for the red No.10 who moves towards the sideline.

No.5 plays the vertical pass and Sahin (18) has the appropriate position to block/intercept it.

Situation 3 - Applying Double Marking High up the Pitch

In this tactical situation, as soon as the pass is directed to No.5, the red left winger (11) drops into a deeper position to provide a passing option.

The defensive midfielder Sahin (18) reads the tactical context and follows the movement.

No.5 passes to No.11 who is under pressure from two players (double marking of No.18 and No.16).

Lewandowski (9) drops back near No.6 in case the ball is directed to him and Mkhitaryan (10) moves near the ball area too.

Creating A Strong Side And Forcing The Ball Wide (Centre Forward Is The First Defender)

When the ball was passed towards the centre back who was positioned on the centre forward's side, Dortmund could create superiority in numbers near the ball area more easily, as the No.10 usually shifted towards the strong side. However, because No.10 shifted across there was no one to apply pressure immediately on the goalkeeper in case of a back pass. So when No.9 applies pressure on the centre back, he also had to prevent the back pass towards the goalkeeper using the correct body shape.

Goalkeeper Passes to the Centre Back on the Centre Forward's Side

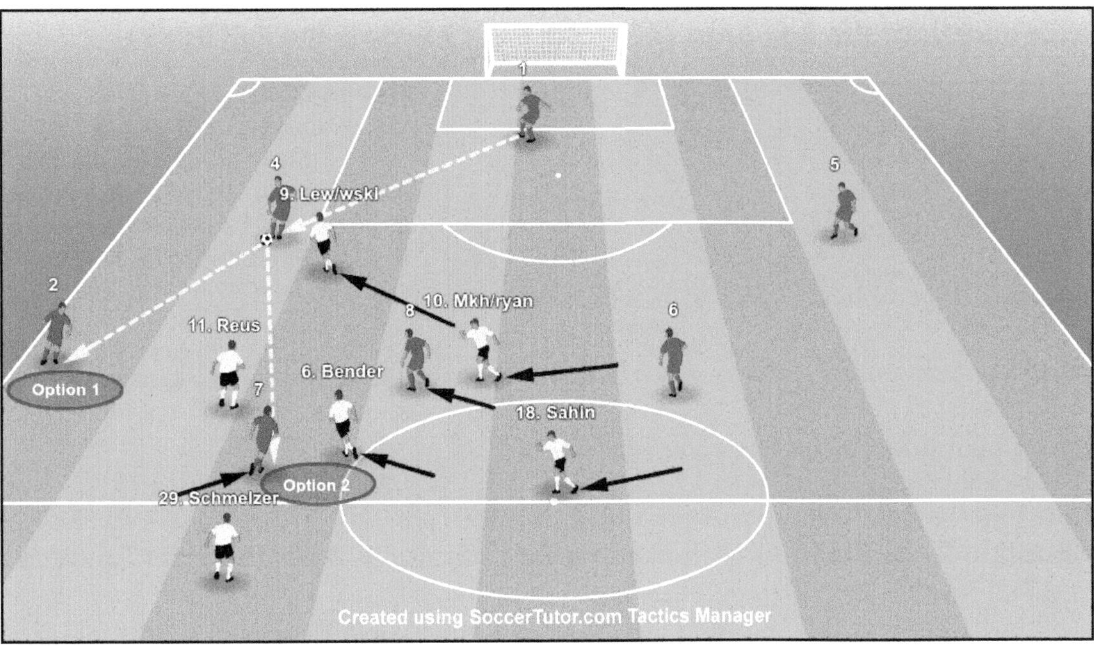

In this situation the goalkeeper's pass is directed to No.4. The centre forward (9) moves immediately to close him down. This time it is important for No.9 to create a strong side by forcing the ball towards the sideline and preventing the pass towards the goalkeeper. This is due to the fact that the No.10 is positioned in a deeper position and is not able to move forward to control the back pass to the goalkeeper. Instead he shifts towards the strong side to create superiority in numbers near the ball area.

No.11 stays in a position which enables him to block the vertical pass and No.6 shifts towards the left to narrow the passing lane. As red No.8 moves towards the potential passing lane, No.6 also moves a few yards forward to be able to control him. The positioning of both No.11 and No.6 prevents the vertical pass (option 2) towards red No.7, so the only available passing option is the one towards the full back No.2 near the sideline (option 1).

Creating Superiority In Numbers And Blocking All Passing Options (Centre Forward Is First Defender)

The main aims after forcing the ball out wide to the full back was marking all potential receivers and creating superiority in numbers around the ball zone. This second aim was easier to achieve on this side as the No.10 (Mkhitaryan) usually shifted towards the strong side and provided an extra man. When pressing on the No.10's side there would not always be a player who would shift across in the same way.

Situation 1 - Marking All Potential Receivers and Creating Superiority in Numbers Near the Ball Area (After the Pass Towards the Full Back)

After the pass towards the full back (2), Reus (11) moves to apply pressure on him. At the same time, the two potential receivers are marked from close distance and No.9 blocks the back pass towards No.4 (all 3 highlighted by circles on diagram). The defensive midfielder (6) moves into a supporting position for No.11 as No.10 is close to red No.8. This is an ideal situation of when Dortmund were carrying out pressing.

Situation 2 - Marking All Potential Passing Options (After the Pass Towards the Full Back)

In this situation Bender (6) moves into an advanced position to mark red No.8 as No.10 is away from the ball area.

This action leaves no opposition player unmarked, but there is no superiority in numbers.

Situation 3 - Marking the Most Dangerous Passing Options (After the Pass Towards the Full Back)

In this situation, the defensive midfielder (6) is in a deep position and No.10 is away from the ball area. After the pass to red No.2, Lewandowski (9) drops back in order to prevent the pass towards red No.8. The only available pass for No.2 is the back pass to No.4 which is the less dangerous one.

ASSESSMENT:

The centre forward (9) and the central attacking midfielder (10) were not always positioned as it is shown in the diagrams (centre forward on the left, central attacking midfielder on the right). During the matches they would switch positions frequently. However, the reaction of the players was always the same.

Tactical Analysis: Creating Superiority In Numbers, Marking All Potential Receivers And Applying Double Marking

The pass is directed to No.4 and Lewandowski (9) moves to put pressure on the ball immediately, creating a strong side.

No.10 and all of Borussia Dortmund's players shift towards the left.

The next pass is towards the red right back (2). The No.10 moves close to the ball area and marks red No.8. Bender (6) does not have to move forward to mark him, but stays in a supporting/covering position to No.11.

No.9 blocks the back pass and No.29 marks red No.7. This reaction leaves no available passing options for the man in possession and Dortmund have an extra man near the ball area.

No.2's pass is directed inside to red No.8 and Mkhitaryan (10) moves to contest him together with No.6 who moves forward and applies double marking.

No.9 drops back and can make it triple marking. As the No.10 shifts near the ball area, Borussia Dortmund manage to create superiority in numbers on the strong side and achieve double marking.

Marking All Potential Receivers After Pass Towards The Full Back (No.10 Is First Defender)

When the ball was directed to the full back, Dortmund's first aim was achieved. However, after this pass the team still had to work hard to win possession. The aims at this stage of pressing were to mark all the potential receivers at a close distance and creating a numerical advantage near the ball area.

As the attack of the opposition took place on the side where Borussia Dortmund's No.10 was positioned, creating superiority in numbers near the ball area was not easily achieved. The main reason for this was that the centre forward (9) usually didn't drop back towards the strong side, but remained in an advanced position. However, when the team had to focus mainly on defending and not on counter attacking, Lewandowski (9) would drop back towards the strong side to create a numerical advantage.

Situation 1 - Marking All Potential Receivers After a Pass Towards the Full Back

As soon as the pass towards the full back near the sideline is made, No.16 applies immediate pressure on him, while all three potential receivers of the ball are being marked from close distance. Specifically, No.10 blocks the potential back pass to No.5 and No.18 together with the right back (26) mark No.6 and No.11 respectively. The defensive midfielder (6) moves towards the strong side and provides balance in midfield.

Situation 2 - Blocking the Most Dangerous Passing Options Near the Ball Area

Here red No.6 did not provide a passing option, so No.18 takes up a supporting position to No.16. After the pass towards red No.3, No.6 moves to receive. As No.18 did not manage to move forward in time, it is No.10's responsibility to prevent a pass between the lines, so he drops back to control red No.6 and block a pass. This reaction leaves the back pass towards No.5 free, but it is the least dangerous pass. No.18 provides superiority in numbers near the ball area and is ready to double mark and the full back (26) marks red No.11 closely.

Tactical Analysis: Blocking The Passing Options

Situation 1 - Marking All Potential Passing Options

The goalkeeper passes to the centre back (5). The red No.6 moves towards the strong side to provide a passing option. Sahin (18) moves forward to control him.

As soon as the pass is directed to No.3 near the sideline, all the potential passing options for the man in possession are marked closely. Sahin (18) marks No.6, No.26 moves close to No.11 and No.10 blocks the back pass to No.5.

As No.18 is in an advanced position, the other defensive midfielder (6) makes an extensive shift towards the strong side to provide balance, support and superiority in numbers.

Situation 2 - Marking the Most Dangerous Passing Options

In this tactical situation, as soon as the pass is directed to the centre back No.5, the red defensive midfielder No.6 drops deeper.

So Borussia Dortmund's defensive midfielder Sahin (18) does not move forward, but instead shifts across to narrow the vertical passing lane.

When red No.5 passes to No.3, the No.6 moves to provide a passing option. So as Sahin (18) is unable to move forward in time to mark him, Mkhitaryan (10) reads the tactical situation and drops to control red No.6 and prevent a pass towards him.

The right back Piszczek (26) marks red No.11 closely and the only available passing option is the back pass towards No.5 which is the less dangerous one.

Situation 3 - Applying Double Marking Near the Sideline

No.5 receives the ball while both the red left back and the left winger are near the sideline.

The red No.6 is too far away to be a potential receiver, so Sahin (18) shifts towards the sideline to block the vertical pass and does not move further forward, but instead stays in a supporting position for Blaszczykowski (16).

After two consecutive passes the ball ends up in No.11's possession near the sideline. Red No.11 is contested by Borussia Dortmund's right back who prevents him from turning. At the same time, Sahin (18) drops back to apply double marking and the two forwards also drop back. All of the other Borussia Dortmund players move towards the strong side.

DEFENDING TACTICAL SITUATION 1

Applying Pressure On the Goalkeeper

Applying Pressure On The Goalkeeper

When one of Borussia Dortmund's forwards put pressure straight on the goalkeeper, his main aim was to create a strong side. The other forward had to make sure that the potential through pass towards the defensive midfielder on the strong side was blocked. These actions made the passes predictable as the players had to play on the strong side.

The centre forward (9) puts pressure on the goalkeeper and forces the ball towards the right giving him two short passing options. The No.10 shifts slightly towards the right so he is ready to apply immediate pressure on No.5 who is the most obvious passing option (option 1). However, he is also aware of the position of No.6 behind him and he does not make an extensive shift, but stays in a position which enables him to control (block) the pass (option 2) towards the opposition's deepest midfielder. Otherwise a successful pass towards No.6 would result in No.9 and No.10 being out of effective defensive positions.

Tactical Analysis: Applying Pressure On The Goalkeeper Against The 4-4-2

The red centre back No.5 passes to No.4 who directs the ball back to the goalkeeper.

No.9 puts pressure on the goalkeeper and blocks the pass to No.4 and No.8 at the same time.

Mkhitaryan (10) takes up a position which enables him to control red No.6 and is he ready to apply pressure for a potential pass to No.5.

The first pass is directed to the red centre back No.5. Mkhitaryan (10) moves to put him under pressure and Lewandowski (9) drops a few yards back into a position which enables him to control the back pass to the goalkeeper.

No.5 passes to the goalkeeper and No.9 moves forward while the No.10 moves towards the inside to prevent a vertical pass. If No.9 is not able to win the ball, he puts pressure on the goalkeeper in a way that forces the ball towards the strong side (circled area). The ball has to be directed towards an area where the Dortmund players already have effective defending positions and there is limited space for the opposition. Otherwise, they would have to shift several yards to get ready to defend on the weak side.

Session For This Tactical Situation *(5 Practices)*

1. Applying Pressure on the Goalkeeper and Forcing the Ball Wide

Objective

To work on applying pressure on the goalkeeper and forcing the ball wide towards the sidelines.

Description

In 1/3 of a full pitch, the goalkeeper passes the ball to one of the centre backs who start positioned on the white cones. As soon as this happens, the closest yellow forward (9 or 10) moves to put pressure on him and force the pass back to the goalkeeper.

The forward (No.9 in diagram) then continuous his run in order to put pressure on the goalkeeper too. His aim is to use his movement and body shape to force the ball towards one side. At the same time, the other forward (No.10 in diagram) takes up a position which enables him to block a vertical pass to the red defensive midfielder No.6 and be close enough to apply immediate pressure on the other centre back (5) when he receives the pass from the goalkeeper (before he manages to dribble the ball through the red cone gate). In addition, when No.9 forces the ball towards one side, he also prevents a potential pass towards the two pole gates (yellow and red).

The centre back does not try to dribble past the yellow forward, but is only allowed to move in a straight line. If the forward catches him before he travels through the gate, he then takes the ball and tries to score together with his teammate within 4 seconds. The same happens if he intercepts a vertical pass towards red No.6.

PROGRESSION

2. Applying Pressure on the Goalkeeper and the Centre Back, Preventing Passes Inside and Forcing the Ball Wide

Objective

To work on applying pressure on the goalkeeper and then on the centre back to prevent inside passes and force the ball wide.

Description

The practice starts with the coach making a long pass from the centre to the goalkeeper who is not allowed to catch the ball with his hands.

The centre forward or the No.10 (they communicate and decide) apply pressure on the goalkeeper and at the same time prevent the pass towards the weak side's centre back inside the light blue zone and the pass through the blue cone gate. At the same time, the other forward should use their movement to prevent the pass towards the red midfielder No.6.

As soon as the goalkeeper passes towards the centre back, the aim of the yellow players is to block the passes towards the blue and red cone gates and force the ball towards the full back (in dark blue zones). As soon as the full back receives he is under the double marking of the winger (No.16 in diagram) and the full back (No.26 in diagram) who try to prevent him from dribbling the ball through the red line of the yellow cone gate. If the yellows win possession they must finish their counter attack within 6-7 seconds. The reds score 2 points if they pass through the white line or dribble through the red line.

PROGRESSION

3. Creating a Strong Side, Forcing the Ball Wide and Marking All Potential Receivers in a 2 Zone Dynamic Practice

Objective

Creating a strong side, forcing the ball wide and marking all potential passing options.

Description

Using an area slightly larger than half a full sized pitch we divide it in two and the teams play 8 v 8 (+ GK). The yellow players start on the red cones and the practice starts with the opposition goalkeeper.

The goalkeeper plays the first pass towards one of the red centre backs and then the game is played on that side and there is a 5 yellows v 4 reds (+ GK) situation. The yellow players try to force the ball wide and win possession while at the same time trying to achieve several other aims.

The aims when the ball is in the centre back's possession:

a. Prevent centre back or def. midfielder (6) from passing through the blue cone gate (1 point for reds).
b. Prevent defensive midfielder (6) from receiving and dribbling the ball through the yellow cone gate or switching play (1 point for the reds).

The aims when the ball reaches the full back:

a. Mark all potential receivers and prevent them from receiving without pressure.
b. Prevent the opposition from retaining possession for more than 4 seconds or from succeeding in making another successful pass to a teammate (1 point).

If the reds dribble the ball through the red end line they score 3 points. The goalkeeper is free to choose whether he passes towards the left or right.

Restrictions

1. The practice takes place on one side only unless the yellow players win possession.
2. Only the two yellow forwards can enter both halves of the pitch.
3. If the yellow players win possession, all players can move freely across both halves, but the yellows have to score within 8-10 seconds.
4. The reds are not allowed to play long balls.

Coaching Points

1. Pressure needs to be applied on the ball carrier very quickly.
2. The other players need to use appropriate positioning, making sure to cover the potential passing options.
3. The focus is always to control the other team by forcing the play out wide towards the sidelines.
4. The players need to be able to read the specific tactical situation (specifically the defensive midfielder who has 2 aims).

PROGRESSION

4. Creating a Strong Side, Forcing The Ball Wide and Marking All Potential Receivers in a 2 Zone Dynamic Practice (2)

Description

This is a progression of the previous practice with the same aims and restrictions for both teams. The only difference is that the reds now try to score in the two mini goals which makes it more difficult for the yellows to defend.

Restriction

The reds are not allowed to use long balls.

PROGRESSION

5. Creating a Strong Side, Forcing The Ball Wide and Marking All Potential Receivers in an 11 v 11 Game

Description

This is a progression of the previous practice and the teams now play 11 v 11 with the same aims and restrictions for both teams.

We add another full sized goal and a goalkeeper for the yellow team. The pitch is still divided so that the reds try to achieve a switch of play, but the players can now move freely across both sides.

DEFENDING TACTICAL SITUATION 2

Defending the Forward Run of the Full Back During the Pressing Application

Defending The Forward Run Of The Full Back During The Pressing Application

When pressing, Borussia Dortmund's players tried to reduce the available time and space for their opponents and especially for the man in possession. When the centre forward or the No.10 put pressure on the centre back near the sideline, Dortmund's winger worked in collaboration with the full back. If the opposition centre back had a few seconds on the ball before he was closed down, the opposition full back would use forward runs to receive in an advanced position. In situations like these when the available time for the man in possession was very short, the Borussia Dortmund winger used to follow the full back until the man in possession was put under pressure.

However, the Borussia Dortmund full back used to stay in a deep position to avoid creating space for the forward moving full back or the opposition forwards. This was generally how the team dealt with the situation. In the examples and the tactical situations here there will be an analysis of how the team dealt with the situation according to the different tactical context.

Situation 1

Red No.5 has space to move forward before No.10 closes him down. No.3 moves forward and No.11 drops back towards the vertical passing lane. Blaszczykowski (16) follows No.3's run as there is an open ball situation and tries to keep the vertical passing lane narrow. Piszczek reads the tactical situation and moves towards the strong side to control No.11 and No.3 in case he moves further forward. The centre back Sokratis (25) shifts towards the right and close to Piszczek (26) to retain the line's cohesion.

No.3 continues his run, but Blaszczykowski (16) stops following him as No.10 has managed to put pressure on the ball. No.3 has now moved forward into No.26's zone of responsibility, so Piszczek has to deal with him and decide whether or not he is going to put pressure on him if No.3 receives the ball. This decision should be made after analysing the position of No.11. In this situation No.11 is positioned towards a narrow passing lane and it is almost impossible for him to receive the ball. He is in a deep position, so if No.3 receives the ball, No.11 will not be able to take advantage of the space behind No.26 and create a 2 v 1 situation before No.25 manages to mark him. So No.26 can focus on No.3 and put pressure on him immediately.

Situation 2

In this situation the red winger No.11 takes up a more advanced position. No.3 again makes a forward run and is followed by Blaszczykowski (16).

As soon as there is pressure on the ball, Blaszczykowski (16) stops following No.3. No.3 enters Piszczek's zone of responsibility again. However, this time Piszczek (26) controls him from a larger distance compared to the previous situation. This is due to the fact that there is already another player (No.11) in his zone of responsibility who can move in behind him and create a 2 v 1 situation. So Piszczek can only focus on No.3 when the centre back Sokratis (25) moves closer to No.11 and takes over his marking.

Tactical Analysis: Defending Against The Forward Run Of The Full Back

Situation 1

No.5 receives and has available space before Mkhitaryan (10) manages to close him down. No.3 moves forward and Blaszczykowski (16) follows his run (he can be a few yards higher up the pitch). This is because even if the ball is directed to No.3, he can take advantage of the transmission phase and close him down before he moves further forward. Piszczek (26) moves into a position which enables him to control both No.11 and No.3 in case he moves further forward.

Mkhitaryan (10) closes No.5 down and Blaszczykowski (16) stops following No.3. However, the red team's centre back (5) manages to pass to No.3 who did not move forward enough to enter Piszczek's (16) zone of responsibility.

Blaszczykowski (16) takes advantage of the transmission phase and closes No.3 down and Piszczek (26) moves to help double mark him. This is because the red No.11 is in a deep position and Sahin (18) can take over his marking.

The other defenders shift across towards the strong side and retain the line's cohesion.

Situation 2

This is a similar situation to the previous one. The only difference is that No.3 has moved into a more advanced position (within No.26's zone of responsibility) and then he receives the pass from No.5. Piszczek (26) takes advantage of the transmission phase and moves to close him down (as soon as the ball leaves No.5's foot). This is because No.11 is in a deep position again and is being marked by Sahin (18). Blaszczykowski (16) moves across to help double mark No.3.

Situation 3

In this similar situation, the difference is that the red No.11 is in an advanced position. No.5 passes to No.3 who receives within Piszczek's (26) zone of responsibility. Piszczek cannot move forward immediately to put pressure on No.3 unless Sokratis (25) takes over No.11's marking. Otherwise No.11 can move in behind him and create a 2 v 1 situation on the flank. So Piszczek waits for Sokratis to move close to No.11 first.

As soon as Sokratis (25) has taken over No.11's marking (there should be communication), Piszczek (26) moves to close the man in possession down. Blaszczykowski (16) helps to apply double marking.

Situation 4

In this tactical situation No.5 plays a long pass into the path of No.3.

This time Piszczek (26) decides to intervene immediately without waiting for Sokratis (25) to mark No.11. This is because he is 100% sure that he is going to reach the ball first and make a clearance.

Session For This Tactical Situation *(4 Practices)*

1. Defending the Forward Run of the Full Back on the Strong Side

Objective

To practice defensive movements to deal with the forward run of the full back on the strong side.

Description

The two teams play 2 v 2 inside the light blue zones, there are 2 red centre backs (4 and 5) in the positions shown and the rest of the players start on the red and yellow cones. The practice starts with the goalkeeper's pass towards a centre back. The yellow No.9 and No.10 move to close down the ball carrier. As soon as he receives, the red full back makes a forward run. The strong side's midfielders of both teams (red 6 and yellow 18 in diagram) enter the light blue zone and create a 3 v 3 situation.

The reds aim to pass through the blue cone gate (towards the red winger) or dribble the ball through it (1 point). They score 3 points if they manage to dribble the ball through the red end line or receive a pass beyond it within the dark blue zone. The yellows try to deal with the forward run of the full back, win possession and then counter attack in an 8 v 8 (+ GK) situation with no zone restrictions.

Restrictions

1. The full back must make a forward run every time the centre back receives the ball from the GK.
2. As soon as the yellows win possession there are no restrictions in regards to the zones, but they have to score within 8-10 seconds.

PROGRESSION

2. Defending the Forward Run of the Full Back on the Strong Side (2)

Description

This is a progression of the previous practice. The aims and restrictions are the same for both teams.

The only difference is that in this practice the red players try to score in the mini goals by shooting from within the light blue zone. This makes it more difficult for the yellow players to defend (and win the ball).

Coaching Points

1. The yellow players must apply pressure on the ball as quickly as possible.
2. The appropriate positioning is needed to prevent the reds from achieving their aims. This includes the correct body shape to block potential passing lanes and the positioning of all players to control the possible passing options.
3. Players need to be able to read the tactical situation and adjust their positioning/movements accordingly.
4. Communication is very important in this practice and the players should use key words (especially between the full back and the winger).

PROGRESSION

3. Defending the Forward Run of the Full Back on the Strong Side in a 10 v 10 Small Sided Game

Created using SoccerTutor.com Tactics Manager

Description

In a 60 X 50 yard area, two teams play a 10 v 10 small sided game. The teams switch roles and each team has the role of the attacking team for 5 minutes. The red defenders and midfielders take up positions on the red cones and the yellow forwards and midfielders on the white cones.

The red team are attacking and the players try to take advantage of the forward run of the full back on the strong side and score (1 point). The yellows have to prevent this, win possession and score within 8-10 seconds (1 point). The reds can also score 1 point if they pass through the cone gate on the strong side or dribble the ball through it. If the ball goes out of play, the game starts with the red goalkeeper.

Restrictions

1. The full back must make a forward run every time the centre back receives the ball from the GK.
2. For the point or goal to count there should be a sequence: Goalkeeper -> Centre back -> Forward pass towards the full back, winger or defensive midfielder.

PROGRESSION

4. Defending the Forward Run of the Full Back on the Strong Side in a Dynamic 11 v 11 Game

Description

The two teams play 11 v 11 in 2/3 of a full pitch. We mark out 2 light blue zones as shown in the diagram.

The practice starts with the red goalkeeper and the red team aim to score against the yellow goalkeeper (3 points). They can also score if they manage to pass or dribble the ball through the yellow cone gate (1 point) after a specific passing sequence: Goalkeeper -> Centre back -> Forward pass.

The final way for the reds to score 1 point is to dribble the ball through the red line on the flanks or receive a pass beyond it within the light blue zone after a successful combination which involves the forward run of the full back.

The yellow players try to prevent these aims, win the ball and then finish their counter attack within 8-10 seconds.

DEFENDING TACTICAL SITUATION 3

Ultra Offensive Pressing

Ultra Offensive Pressing

In some periods of specific matches, Borussia Dortmund used ultra offensive pressing. This way of pressing was carried out when their aim was to reduce the available time and space even more for the opposition defenders, despite the fact that the 2 forwards (No.10 and No.9) were forced to take up central positions due to the opposition defensive midfielder who had a deep position.

This kind of pressing was used against teams with full backs who used to play in advanced positions. This central positioning of Borussia Dortmund's forwards did not enable them to apply immediate pressure on the centre backs who had taken up wide positions, so the winger moved a few yards forward in between the centre backs and the full backs.

Starting Positions Against the 4-4-2 Formation

Borussia Dortmund's players take up positions in order to apply ultra offensive pressing and reduce the available time on the ball for the man in possession. These positions were taken when the opposition played with a defensive midfielder in a deeper central position and the 2 centre backs took up wide positions. As the forwards (10 and 9) were forced to take up central positions to prevent the vertical pass to the defensive midfielder (6), the wingers (11 and 16) moved a few yards forward and took up balanced positions between the advanced full back and the centre back. This position enabled them to move back and close down the full back in case there was a long pass from the goalkeeper and also apply immediate pressure on the centre back if the pass was directed to him.

Applying Immediate Pressure, Forcing The Ball Inside & Preventing A Pass To The Full Back

When the winger decided to put pressure on the centre back, his direct opponent was left unmarked. This meant that the winger had to put pressure on the centre back immediately before the centre back was able to turn towards Borussia Dortmund's goal with his head up and with a view of the full pitch. This meant the winger could prevent a potential pass to his direct opponent (who is left unmarked) and force the ball towards the inside.

The defensive midfielder on the strong side (No.18 in diagram) together with the No.10 tried to prevent the through passes towards a player (link player) who could direct the ball to the advanced full back.

Situation 1

In this situation Dortmund's players are not as focused on marking the players, but are mainly focussed on blocking the passing lanes. No.16 has moved away from his direct opponent No.3 who is left free near the sideline. The aim of the players is to reduce the available time and space for the opposition and prevent either the direct pass towards No.3 or an indirect one via a link player.

The goalkeeper passes to No.5 and as soon as the ball leaves his foot, Blaszczykowski (16) moves to take advantage of the transmission phase and put pressure on the new man in possession. The aim of this is to deny No.5 available time on the ball and prevent him from turning towards Boussia Dortmund's goal and force him towards his own goal.

If No.5 does manage to turn, Blaszczykowski applies pressure in a way (with the correct body shape) that blocks the pass towards his direct opponent No.3 who has been left free without marking.

As the ball is forced towards the inside, the centre forward (9) moves into a position which enables him to control both the back pass to the goalkeeper and the pass to the deep positioned defensive midfielder (6). Mkhitaryan (10) blocks the pass towards the inside and the strong side's defensive midfielder Sahin (18) moves to block the potential vertical pass and also control the full back No.3 in case he receives.

Borussia Dortmund's right back Piszczek (26) moves forward with the aim of controlling both No.11 and a potential forward pass to No.3. Finally, the positioning of the weak side's winger Reus (11) is important as he controls a potential long pass towards No.4 or No.2.

Situation 2

In this situation the red midfielder No.6 tries to move towards a potential passing lane in order to receive a through pass. This is a dangerous pass as he can be a link player to move the ball to the full back who is free. So Sahin (18) has to block the pass towards him as well as the pass towards No.11. No.9 shifts into a position that enables him to both control a pass to the goalkeeper and to block a risky through pass towards No.8.

Situation 3

In this situation, as soon as the centre back (5) receives he is put under immediate pressure and is forced towards the inside.

No.5 passes back to the goalkeeper who moves towards the strong side to provide a passing option.

The goalkeeper is being put under pressure by the centre forward (9) and Mkhitaryan (10) blocks the through pass and controls No.6 at the same time. The goalkeeper is forced to play a long ball under this pressure.

Situation 4

No.5 receives and is forced towards the inside. He tries to make a through pass to No.10, but because he is under heavy pressure from No.16 and Sahin (18) has the correct positioning, the pass is intercepted.

Situation 5

No.5 receives and as he moves towards the inside under Blaszczykowski's (16) pressure, he manages to make an inside pass towards the weak side's defensive midfielder. However, this is not a very dangerous option.

As Reus (11) is not close enough to close No.8 down immediately, he receives without pressure and moves forward.

Mkhitaryan (10) moves to close down No.8 while the rest of the players drop back as there is an open ball situation. This results in them trying to get into a compact and correct shape.

Situation 6

In this situation, No.5 decides to play a long pass (switch) towards the weak side's centre back (4).

Reus (11) has to read the situation and decide if he can move early enough to intercept the ball or force the centre back into making a mistake. If he thinks he will be too late, he should stay in his position.

Session For This Tactical Situation *(3 Practices)*

1. Pressing High Up the Pitch, Forcing the Ball Inside and Blocking Potential Passes

Objective

To work on pressing high up the pitch, forcing the ball towards the inside and blocking the potential diagonal and vertical passes.

Description

In 1/3 of a full sized pitch, there are 2 mini goals, 4 cone gates (illustrated by red dashed lines) in the centre and 2 yellow zones with the red full backs inside. The yellow players take up the positions indicated by the blue cones.

The practice starts as soon as the goalkeeper passes the ball towards one of the red centre backs. As soon as the ball leaves his foot, the winger on the strong side (No. 17 in diagram) puts pressure on the man in possession and forces the ball towards the inside (preventing a pass towards the full back).

The other players try to block the potential passes towards the 3 goals on the strong side. Passing through the yellow cone gate scores 1 point, passing through the red cone gate scores 2 points and passing into the mini goal scores 5 points. Passing to the full back who must receive within the yellow zone is also worth 5 points.

When the yellow players win possession, they try to score within 5 seconds against the 4 red defenders who should drop back quickly and defend.

Restriction

The red players are not allowed to pass the ball back to the goalkeeper.

Coaching Points

1. The yellow players need to apply immediate pressure on the ball so they can win it and take advantage of the positive transition (counter attack) before the other defenders have time to get back.
2. The first player to close down the red centre back should use their body shape to force the pass towards the inside, instead of one side of the pitch.
3. Appropriate positioning with good communication is needed so potential passing options are blocked.
4. There is a need for quick and accurate finishing.

PROGRESSION

2. Pressing High Up the Pitch, Forcing the Ball Inside and Blocking Potential Passes in a Dynamic Zonal Game

Description

This is a multi-purpose practice and we use half a full sized pitch. The two teams play 8 v 8 (+ GK). The game starts with the red goalkeeper's pass towards one of the centre backs. As soon as this happens the practice takes place in the strong side's light blue zone and the central area only.

The red players try to move the ball towards the full back on the strong side within the yellow zone (1 point). If this is achieved, the next aim is to try and score by dribbling the ball through the red line or receiving a pass beyond it within the white zone (3 points). If the reds pass to a midfielder in the centre, they try to score in the mini goals (3 points). The players are not allowed to pass to the other side.

A pass back to the goalkeeper can be made within the dark blue zone and if this happens, the centre forward (9) must apply pressure and force him to make a rushed pass. If the goalkeeper switches play 1 point is scored. The yellows try to stop the reds achieving their aims by blocking the passing lanes, pressuring the ball carrier using the correct body shape, winning the ball and finishing their counter within 8-10 seconds. If the yellows win possession there are no restrictions in regards to the zones.

Coaching Points

1. The players need to use good cohesion and communication to block the available passing lanes.
2. When closing down the ball carrier, correct body shape must be used to force the pass to one side.

PROGRESSION

3. Pressing High Up the Pitch, Forcing the Ball Inside and Blocking Potential Passes in a Dynamic 11 v 11 Zonal Game

Description

In 2/3 of a full sized pitch, two teams play 11 v 11. The game starts with the red goalkeeper and the yellow players take up position on the blue cones in order to apply ultra offensive pressing.

The game starts with the red goalkeeper passing to one of the centre backs. The reds try to score against the goalkeeper (3 points) but if they manage to move the ball to the full back on the strong side (yellow zone) they score 2 points. If they move the ball to one of their teammates in the light blue zone, they score another 2 points. They can also score 2 points if they pass to a midfielder who then makes a successful pass into the light blue zone.

The yellow players try to apply immediate pressure on the centre back, force the ball inside and block the available passing options. When they win possession, they must score within 8-10 seconds.

Restriction

The goalkeeper can only receive a back pass within the dark blue zone on the strong side.

DEFENDING TACTICAL SITUATION 4

Ultra Offensive Pressing: Defending Against a Long Pass Towards the Advanced Full Back

Defending Against A Long Pass Towards The Advanced Full Back

In situations when ultra offensive pressing was used, there were times when the opposition managed to direct the ball to the full back in an advanced positioned. Borussia Dortmund triggered specific mechanisms to deal with these particular situations.

Situation 1

The goalkeeper plays a long ball towards red No.3. The winger Blaszczykowski (16) takes advantage of the transmission phase in order to close the new man in possession down. The full back Piszczek (26) shifts towards the right but stays close to his direct opponent No.11. The strong side's defensive midfielder Sahin (18) provides support. With this reaction balance is retained for Dortmund.

Situation 2

In this situation No.16 is in a more advanced position and is unable to close No.3 who receives the long ball. The defensive midfielder Sahin (18) is the player who takes over the role of closing down the ball carrier and No.16 drops back into a supporting position. As the man in possession has available time on the ball before Sahin manages to close him down, an open ball situation is created. Red No.11 moves forward to receive and Dortmund's full back (26) follows his run to prevent him from receiving in behind.

Situation 3

No.17 is in an advanced position and unable to put pressure on red No.3. The red winger (11) has dropped back into a deeper position within Sahin's (18) zone of responsibility. So when the long ball is played to No.3, the right back (26) takes advantage of the transmission phase (he has no direct opponent) and moves to close the new man in possession down. Sahin takes over No.11's marking and Aubameyang (17) drops back to help double mark him.

Situation 4

No.17 is in an advanced position and unable to close No.3 down again. The only difference is that red No.11 is in an advanced position. Sokratis (25) is close enough to take over No.11's marking so Piszczek (26) moves forward to pressure red No.3 again. The defensive midfielder on the weak side (6) drops back to prevent a 3v3 situation.

ASSESSMENT:

The collaboration between defenders, which has the form of a chain reaction, can only be carried out if the distances between the defenders are short.

Tactical Analysis: Applying Immediate Pressure And Defending A Long Pass Towards The Advanced Full Back

Situation 1

The goalkeeper passes to the centre back (5) and Blaszczykowski (16) moves to close him down immediately and blocks the pass towards No.3 at the same time.

The defensive midfielder Sahin (18) moves into a covering position and controls No.3 as well.

No.5 passes back to the goalkeeper and Lewandowski (9) moves to pressure him. Mkhitaryan (10) shifts to prevent the vertical pass to red No.6. The goalkeeper plays a long ball towards the full back No.3 and the defensive midfielder Sahin (18) moves to close the new man in possession down.

Blaszczykowski (16) drops back to provide support and No.6 moves into a position which provides balance in midfield.

Situation 2

In this situation the right winger (16) is in an advanced position again and is unable to close No.3 down. However, the red No.11 has dropped back into a deep position, so as soon as the long pass towards No.3 has been made, Piszczek (26) has no opponent to mark so can move forward and close No.3 down. Blaszczykowski (16) moves to help double mark him.

Situation 3

In this situation red No.11 has an advanced position. However, as the Dortmund defenders retain short distances between each other and Sokratis (25) is close enough to take over red No.11's marking immediately, Piszczek (26) decides to move forward again and close No.3 down. The defensive midfielder (6) drops to prevent a 3v3 situation at the back.

Session For This Tactical Situation *(4 Practices)*

1. Defensive Reactions to a Successful Long Pass Towards the Advanced Full Back with High Tempo Pressing

Objective

To develop ultra offensive pressing when dealing with a successful long pass towards the full back.

Description

Using a full sized pitch, the coach starts the practice by passing to the goalkeeper. The goalkeeper receives and moves to the right or left before playing either a long pass towards the full back within the yellow zone (diagram 1) or a 1-2 combination with the centre back followed by a long pass towards the full back (diagram 2).

The full back's yellow zone is divided into a high and a low section. There are also 2 blue zones (one light and one dark blue) on each side. These areas help the defensive midfielder and the full back on that side to decide how to deal with the situation:

1. If the ball is directed to the low part of the full back's yellow area, the winger moves to contest him.
2. If the ball is directed to the high part of the full back's yellow area and the red winger is inside the dark blue zone, the defensive midfielder moves to contest the full back and the winger moves to cover (as shown in diagram 1).
3. In the same situation as 2, if the red winger is deeper inside the light blue zone, the full back moves to contest No.2 and the defensive midfielder moves to cover.
4. If the winger is out of position (diagram 2) either the full back or the winger (depending on the red winger's position) moves to contest the man in possession.

Coaching Points

1. The yellow players must apply pressure on the ball to take advantage of the transmission phase.
2. Players need to be able to read the tactical situation and adjust their positioning/movements accordingly.
3. Communication is very important in this practice and the players should use key words.

PROGRESSION

2. Defending a Successful Long Pass with Cohesive Pressing on the Strong Side in a 9 v 8 (+GK) Practice

Description

In a 60 x 50 yard area, the practice starts with the red goalkeeper in possession who moves towards the sideline with the ball and either makes a long pass or plays a short pass to a centre back. With the short pass, once the yellow players press the ball, the centre back passes back to the goalkeeper who then directs the ball towards the full back on the strong side.

The reds score a goal if they manage to dribble the ball through the red line or receive a pass beyond it within the dark blue zone. This must be after a successful combination which involves a long pass (by the goalkeeper) towards the full back in the yellow zone.

The yellow players try to deal successfully with the situation with cohesive reactions, win the ball and then finish their counter attack within 8-10 seconds.

Restrictions

1. The long pass from the goalkeeper should always be directed to the full back on the strong side.
2. If the ball goes out of play, the yellow players return to their starting positions and the game starts again with the red goalkeeper.

PROGRESSION

3. Defending a Successful Long Pass with Cohesive Pressing on the Strong Side in a 9 v 8 (+GK) Practice (2)

Description

This is a progression of the previous practice. The same rules and restrictions apply.

This time the reds can also score in the mini goals positioned outside the dark blue zones. This makes it more difficult for the yellow players to defend and increases the urgency required to close down the ball carrier and block the passing lanes.

PROGRESSION

4. Defending a Successful Long Pass With Cohesive Pressing on the Strong Side in an 11 v 11 Game

Description

This is another progression and the two teams now play an 11 v 11 game.

The red team try to score against the yellow goalkeeper in the full sized goal. However, if they manage to use a successful combination which involves a long pass towards the full back, the goal counts as 3 goals.

The yellow team try to win possession and then finish their counter attack within 8-10 seconds. If the ball goes out of play, the yellow players return to their starting positions and the game starts again with the red goalkeeper.

CHAPTER 3

PRESSING AGAINST THE 4-3-3

Pressing Against The 4-3-3 Formation

When playing against the 4-3-3 formation, the main problem during the pressing application came from the deep position of the opposition defensive midfielder. When this player managed to receive behind the two forwards and the strong side's attacking midfielder is in an advanced position, the opposition could create problems for Borussia Dortmund. In order for the team to deal with this potential problem, the players reacted in two main ways which are presented in the following diagrams.

Starting Positions Against the 4-3-3 Formation

In this diagram the starting positions against a 4-3-3 formation are shown.

The two forwards (9 and 10) take up central positions to deal with the opposition defensive midfielder (6).

Putting Pressure on the Goalkeeper Against the 4-3-3 Formation

When the opposition played with a 4-3-3 formation and one of Borussia Dortmund's forwards (9 or 10) decided to put pressure on the goalkeeper, the other forward had to make sure that the through pass towards the defensive midfielder (6) was not possible. He then tried to take up the most suitable position so he is able to put pressure on the centre back as soon as possible.

When the forward decided to put pressure straight on the goalkeeper (and use good body shape to close off one side), the No.10 had to take up a position which enabled him to block the potential pass towards the defensive midfielder (6) and also control the potential pass to the centre back (5). If the ball was directed to the centre back, No.10 would be close enough to put pressure on him as soon as possible.

Tactical Analysis: Putting Pressure On The Goalkeeper Against The 4-3-3 Formation

Reus (11) forces the red centre back (4) to pass back to the goalkeeper.

As soon as this takes place, Lewandowski (9) puts pressure on the goalkeeper and Mkhitaryan (10) takes up a position to control No.5 and block the potential pass to No.6.

The goalkeeper passes towards the defensive midfielder (6) and Mkhitaryan (10) blocks the pass.

Blocking The Vertical / Inside Passes And Forcing The Ball Wide

As like the team did against the 4-4-2 formation, when the goalkeeper made the first pass towards the centre back near the sideline, the aim for Borussia Dortmund was to prevent the short passing options, except for the pass towards the full back.

The First Pass is Towards the Centre Back

In this situation, the ball is passed to the centre back positioned on the same side as Mkhitaryan (10). Borussia Dortmund's players try to force the ball towards the sideline (option 1) by blocking the vertical pass to the red winger (11) who takes up a position behind Sahin (18) and between the lines (option 2). This is obtained by the shifting of the defensive midfielder Sahin towards the strong side. As the red No.6 is too far away to provide a passing option, there is no available passing option towards the inside.

In this diagram there is a slight variation to the previous situation.

The only difference is that the red No.6 provides another passing option (option 3) for the man in possession.

Defending The Inside Pass Towards The Def. Midfielder (No.10 Is First Defender)

When the No.10 (Mkhitaryan) put pressure on the centre back during the pressing application against the 4-3-3 formation, there was often a problem which arose from the positioning of the defensive midfielder (No.6 in diagram) and the attacking midfielder (No.10 in diagram) on the strong side.

Specifically, when the defensive midfielder (6) was an available passing option and the attacking midfielder on the strong side (10) took up a position behind Dortmund's defensive midfielder (18), superiority in numbers (2 v 1) against the full back was created. This situation was dealt with in two main ways.

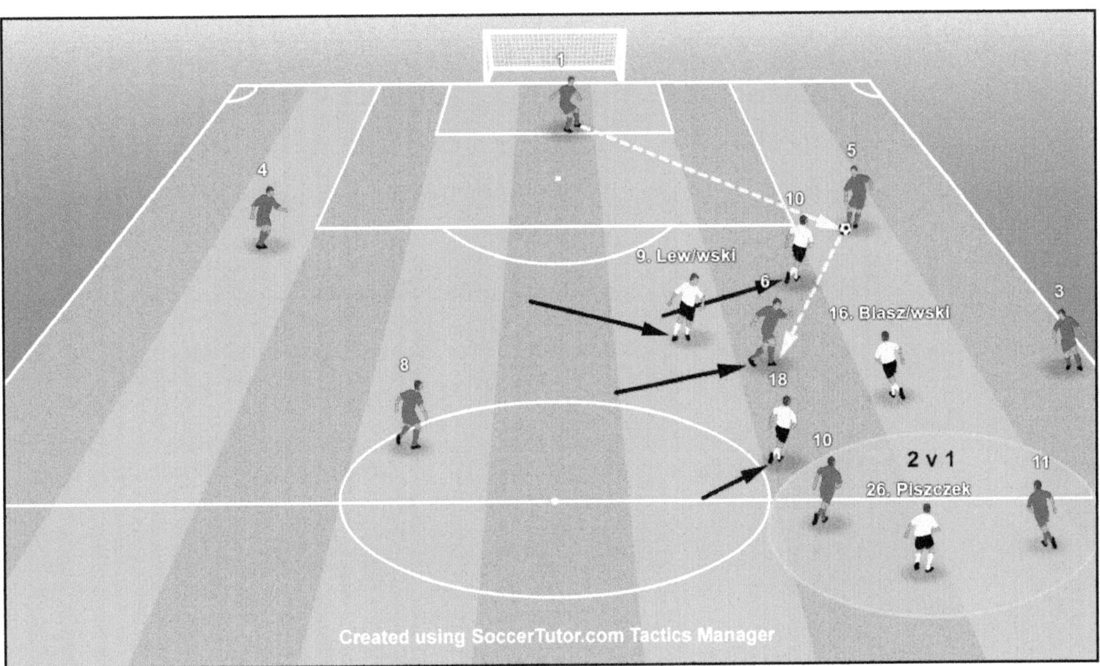

This situation shows the main problem that Dortmund had when playing against the 4-3-3 formation. The red defensive midfielder (6) shifts towards the strong side and provides a passing option and the red No.10 on the strong side has an advanced position between the lines. This is a difficult situation during the pressing application as the positioning of the red No.10 creates a 2 v 1 situation against Piszczek (26). Sahin (18) takes up a position which ensures compactness between the defenders and the midfielders. This positioning enables him to be able move back and track No.10 if needed, thus preventing the 2 v 1 numerical advantage for the reds.

However, if Sahin is forced to move into an advanced position, the distance between him and No.10 will grow and there might be a problem on the right. One option Dortmund used to deal with this situation was for the centre forward to drop into a deeper position and towards the strong side in order to control No.6. It is then necessary for No.10 to create a strong side and prevent a back pass towards the goalkeeper. This situation is shown in the diagram above.

As soon as the pass is directed to red No.6, Lewandowski (9) moves to put him under pressure. In this situation, it is not possible to be apply pressure immediately, so No.6 is able to receive and then face Borussia Dortmund's goal.

However, because Sahin (18) is not forced to move forwards, he can stay in his position and remain close to red No.10. Blaszczykowski (16) shifts towards the inside to block the through pass to either No.10 or No.11.

Tactical Analysis: Forcing The Ball Wide Against The 4-3-3 Formation

Situation 1 - **Dealing with an Inside Pass Towards the Defensive Midfielder (1)**

The pass is directed to No.5 and all the Dortmund players move towards the strong side. Red No.10 is in between the lines and behind Sahin (18). The aim of the players is to force the ball towards the sideline (which is why the vertical pass towards No.10 is blocked). The right back Piszczek (26) reads the tactical situation and does not move forward, but stays in a position to control both No.10 and No.11 (the only way for the reds to direct the ball to these players is to use a long pass).

Red No.6 receives and Lewandowski (9) moves to close him down. Dortmund's midfielders drop back and leave him to contest No.6. However, they get compact in order to block the vertical pass towards No.10 and No.11.

The player in possession (6) is forced towards the sideline, facing away from goal.

No.6 is forced to pass to the left back No.3 near the sideline. As soon as the pass is made, Blaszczykowski (16) moves to apply pressure, Piszczek (26) marks No.11 closely and Sahin (18) drops into a supporting position. Mkhitaryan (10) moves to block the back pass and because Lewandowski (9) also marks red No.6, the available passing options for the red team have been reduced and Borussia Dortmund are very likely to regain possession.

Situation 2 - Dealing with an Inside Pass Towards the Defensive Midfielder (2)

This is another option for how Borussia Dortmund deal with a similar situation. No.9 is now too away from being able to put pressure on red No.6. However, the short distance between Sahin (18) and red No.6 enables the defensive midfielder to move immediately forward and close No.6 down before he can get his head up. It is important that Sahin moves forward as soon as the ball leaves No.5's foot and not any earlier.

Situation 3 - Dealing with an Inside Pass Towards the Defensive Midfielder (3)

No.5 receives the pass from the goalkeeper and Mkhitaryan (10) moves to put him under pressure.

Red No.6 shifts towards the strong side to provide a passing option and Lewandowski (9) is too far away to be able to control him.

Before No.5's pass, Sahin (18) reads the tactical situation (No.9 away from No.6, short distance between him and No.6) so as soon as the pass towards red No.6 is made, he moves immediately to close him down. His main aim is to prevent him from passing forward. Secondly he tries to force him back or make him pass back. Lewandowski and Mkhitaryan move towards the ball zone to take advantage of Sahin's potential intervention.

Situation 4 - Dealing with an Inside Pass Towards the Defensive Midfielder (4)

In this example we show how the early movement of Sahin (18) towards red No.6 can create more problems. This is because Sahin's distance from No.10 grows, so if No.5 directs the ball to No.10 instead of No.6, this will enable the red team to take advantage of the 2 v 1 situation (highlighted in diagram).

Tactical Analysis: Defending A Long Pass To The No.10 Against The 4-3-3 Formation

Situation 1 - Early Movement Causes Problems

After the goalkeeper's pass to No.5, No.6 moves to provide a passing option. Borussia Dortmund's defensive midfielder Sahin (18) moves forward to mark him.

This creates space behind Sahin which is available for red No.10 if he receives an accurate pass. No.5 plays a long pass towards No.10.

As the pass from No.5 is accurate, No.10 receives and turns. Piszczek (26) decides to drop back instead of making a risky move to put pressure on the man in possession.

All of Borussia Dortmund's defenders also drop back to give time to the midfielders to close the man in possession (10) down. So the application of pressing from Borussia Dortmund was not successful in this instance.

Situation 2 - Dealing with the Long Pass Towards the No.10 (1)

This is a similar situation to the previous one. The only difference is that Sahin (18) does not move into an advanced position, but instead stays close to his teammates.

This means that Sahin is close to red No.10 and does not leave much available space for him.

The long pass towards No.10 is accurate, but the short distance between Sahin (18) and the red No.10 enables Sahin to drop a few yards back during the transmission phase and head the ball clear.

Situation 3 - Dealing with the Long Pass Towards the No.10 (2)

In this similar situation Sahin (18) is not able to head the ball clear, but he is able to drop back and contest the new man in possession before he finds time to make an accurate forward pass.

Situation 4 - The No.10 Drops Deep to Receive

In this situation red No.6 is further away from the ball area. The strong side's attacking midfielder (the No.10) drops back to offer a passing option.

Sahin (18) can focus on marking him as well as narrowing the vertical passing option. This is because Piszczek (26) does not have two players to deal with.

As soon as the pass is directed to red No.10, three Borussia Dortmund players all move to mark the new man in possession (triple marking).

Lewandowski (9) moves to block the horizontal pass towards No.6.

Creating A Strong Side And Forcing The Ball Wide (Centre Forward Is First Defender)

When the centre forward was the first defender, the previous situation was not much of a problem. The No.10 would shift across towards the strong side and close to the opposition No.6, which enables Bender (6) to stay in a deep position within his zone of responsibility.

The First Pass is Towards the Centre Back on the Centre Forward's Side

If the ball was directed towards the side where the centre forward (9) was positioned, Lewandowski was the first player to put pressure on the ball. The aim was again for Borussia Dortmund to force the ball wide.

The central position of the No.10 (Mkhitaryan) enables him to move quickly towards the strong side and control a potential pass (option 3) towards No.6. With this action Bender (6) is not forced to leave his zone of responsibility to put pressure on red No.6, but instead stays close to his teammates.

Furthermore, there are no other available short passing options for the man in possession except the pass towards No.2. So it is easier to apply pressing on this side if No.9 manages to create a strong side and block the pass back to the goalkeeper.

Forcing The Ball Wide And Marking All The Potential Receivers Of The Ball

After two consecutive passes, the ball ends up with red No.2. The left winger Reus (11) moves to put him under pressure.

The rest of the Borussia Dortmund players shift towards the strong side and mark all the potential receivers including the pass back towards red No.4.

CHAPTER 4

PRESSING AGAINST THE 3-4-3

Pressing Against The 3-4-3 Formation

Borussia Dortmund had to deal with the 3-4-3 formation mainly when teams which used the 4-3-3 formation would switch to this specific formation by dropping their defensive midfielder into a centre back's position.

Starting Positions Against the 3-4-3 Formation

The two Borussia Dortmund forwards (No.9 and No.10) had to take up wider positions against the 3-4-3 formation. This was because there was no midfielder behind them who had to be under control.

The two forwards would shift slightly towards the sidelines so they were able to control all three defenders.

Putting Pressure On The Goalkeeper Against The 3-4-3 Formation

When putting pressure on the GK against the 3-4-3 formation the deeper positioned forward (No.10 in diagram) took up a position to control two defenders as the pass towards the third one was blocked.

Additionally, there was no need to focus on preventing the through ball as the defensive midfielders had the responsibility of marking the midfielders who were potential receivers of the ball.

The centre forward (9) moves to put pressure on the goalkeeper and prevent a potential pass to red No.4 at the same time. Mkhitaryan (10) has to then deal with both red No.6 and No.5, so he has to take up a position which enables him to put pressure on both of them as soon as they receive a pass (as shown in the diagram above).

Tactical Analysis: Putting Pressure On The Goalkeeper

Situation 1

Red No.4 is forced to pass back to the goalkeeper in this situation.

Lewandowski (9) moves to put pressure on him and Mkhitaryan (10) takes up a suitable position to control both red No.6 and No.5.

The goalkeeper passes to red No.6 and Mkhitaryan (10) shifts to prevent the vertical pass and force the ball towards the sideline.

The rest of the Borussia Dortmund players shift towards the right so they are ready to defend, while Sahin (18) not only shifts, but also marks red No.10 who is a potential receiver of the ball.

As soon as the pass towards No.5 is made, Mkhitaryan moves to put him under pressure. Sahin shifts to block the potential vertical pass in collaboration with No.16. The other players shift towards the right. No.26 does not move to mark red No.11 as the passing lane towards him is very narrow and it is unlikely he receives. This reaction reduces the available time and space for the man in possession, forces the ball towards the sidelines and limits the opposition's passing options.

Situation 2

This is a similar situation to the previous one. The goalkeeper passes to No.5. Mkhitaryan (10) moves to close the man in possession down. The red No.10 moves towards the ball area and provides a passing option. So Sahin (18) moves to not only block the vertical pass, but also to mark red No.10.

No.3 moves forward and No.11 drops back. Dortmund's players do not follow their direct opponents, but defend the space. This reaction happens because the vertical pass is blocked and the man in possession does not have enough time on the ball to make an accurate pass.

Blocking The Vertical / Inside Passes And Forcing The Ball Wide

As against the other formations, when the first pass was made towards the centre back, the players tried to prevent all the passes except for the one towards the full back near the sideline.

The goalkeeper's pass is directed straight to red No.5. Mkhitaryan (10) moves to put him under pressure and create a strong side (blocking the back pass). The red team are thus forced to play on the strong side.

Borussia Dortmund's aim is then to force the pass towards the full back. That is why Blaszczykowski (16) and Sahin (18) try to narrow the passing lane towards red No.11 (option 2). Sahin (the defensive midfielder) also has a second aim as he must prevent the inside pass to red No.10 (option 3).

Tactical Analysis: Forcing The Ball Wide After The First Pass To The Centre Back

Situation 1

In this situation No.5 is put under pressure by Mkhitaryan (10). The red No.10 moves towards the ball area, but he is being blocked by Mkhitaryan and unable to receive a pass.

Sahin (18) is focused on narrowing the vertical passing lane in collaboration with Blaszczykowski (16). With this reaction, the ball is forced towards red No.3.

Situation 2

This time the red No.10 moves into an available passing lane.

Sahin (18) moves not only to narrow the vertical passing lane, but also to mark No.10.

ASSESSMENT:

As it appears from the analysis above, when Borussia Dortmund had to apply pressing against a team that used the 3-4-3 formation, not many things were changed compared to when pressing against the 4-4-2 formation.

Ultra Offensive Pressing

When Borussia Dortmund wanted to reduce the available time and space for the opposition defenders, the players adjusted their positions in order to be able to apply ultra offensive pressing.

Starting Positions Against the 3-4-3 Formation

In the diagram above we show the positions of Borussia Dortmund's players when their aim was to apply ultra offensive pressing. As the centre forward (9) takes up an advanced position on the left, the opposition goalkeeper is forced to pass to either red No.6 or No.5.

The right winger (16) moves a few yards forward to reduce the distance between No.5 and himself. Sahin (18) shifts towards the right to be able to control No.3 in case the ball is directed to him.

Putting Immediate Pressure On The Ball And Forcing The Ball Inside

The application of ultra offensive pressing did not change significantly compared to the application against the 4-4-2 formation.

Preventing the Pass to the Full Back after the First Pass to the Centre Back

In this situation Borussia Dortmund's players are not focused on marking the players, but on blocking the passing lanes.

However, as one of their main aims is to prevent the pass towards the full back No.3, the red No.10 moves towards the ball area to become a link player. Sahin's (18) reaction is to move close to him and mark him, but he is still in a position to control red No.3.

Tactical Analysis: Forcing The Ball Wide After The First Pass Towards The Centre Back

Situation 1

Blaszczykowski (16) takes advantage of the transmission phase and moves to put pressure on the ball immediately. At the same time, the red No.10 moves towards the ball area to provide a passing option.

Sahin (18) reads the tactical situation and as he has to make sure that the ball will not be passed to red No.3, he marks No.10 from the outside (not a goal side position).

Red No.5 passes to No.10 and Sahin (18) puts pressure on him in a way that prevents the pass towards the left back No.3.

Mkhitaryan (10) drops back to help apply double marking from the inside and Blaszczykowski (16) also moves near the ball area.

If the reds manage to pass to the full back, Dortmund retain balance as the defensive midfielder moves to close the new man in possession down, while the winger drops into a defensive midfielder's position. If the winger is advanced enough, it is necessary for the attacking midfielder to shift into a defensive midfielder's position.

Situation 2

The goalkeeper passes to No.5 and the red No.10 drops into a deeper position.

Sahin (18) does not follow No.10, because if he does he will not be able to control No.3 in case he receives.

Sahin communicates with Mkhitaryan (10) who shifts across to take over red No.10's marking.

No.5 passes to No.10 and Mkhitaryan (10) moves to put pressure on him, while Sahin (18) shifts across to block the passing lane to No.3.

Blaszczykowski (16) drops back to help double mark the red No.10, who is thus unable to turn towards Borussia Dortmund's goal. He is also unable to pass to red No.3 as Sahin is blocking the pass.

ASSESSMENT:

All the other options of how to deal with the problems that can rise during ultra offensive pressing application are similar to the situations presented against the 4-4-2 formation.

During the matches they would switch positions frequently. However the reaction of the players was the same.

CHAPTER 5

DEFENDING IN THE MIDDLE THIRD

Defending In The Middle Third

Borussia Dortmund are one of the best counter attacking sides in the world. For the team to be able to use their counter attacking tactics, there needs to be available space to take advantage of. In most matches, they used a mixed way of defending. The first was to wait for the opposition to enter the middle third, but this type of defending was interrupted by sudden efforts of pressing high up the pitch.

When defending within the middle third, the team used zonal defending and all players played at a very high tempo. ***Jurgen Klopp*** admitted that he was influenced by the great ***Arrigo Sacchi*** when applying these kinds of tactics. Every player applied great pressure to the opponent within their zone of responsibility to reduce his available time and space. The players tried to keep the team compact by maintaining short distances between the three lines as well as cohesion within the lines (especially the defensive one) by retaining short distances between the players within the line.

Every time there was a pass towards an opponent positioned between the lines, they were put under great pressure immediately, in order to prevent him from turning towards Borussia Dortmund's goal.

Keeping a Compact Formation (30 x 45 Yards)

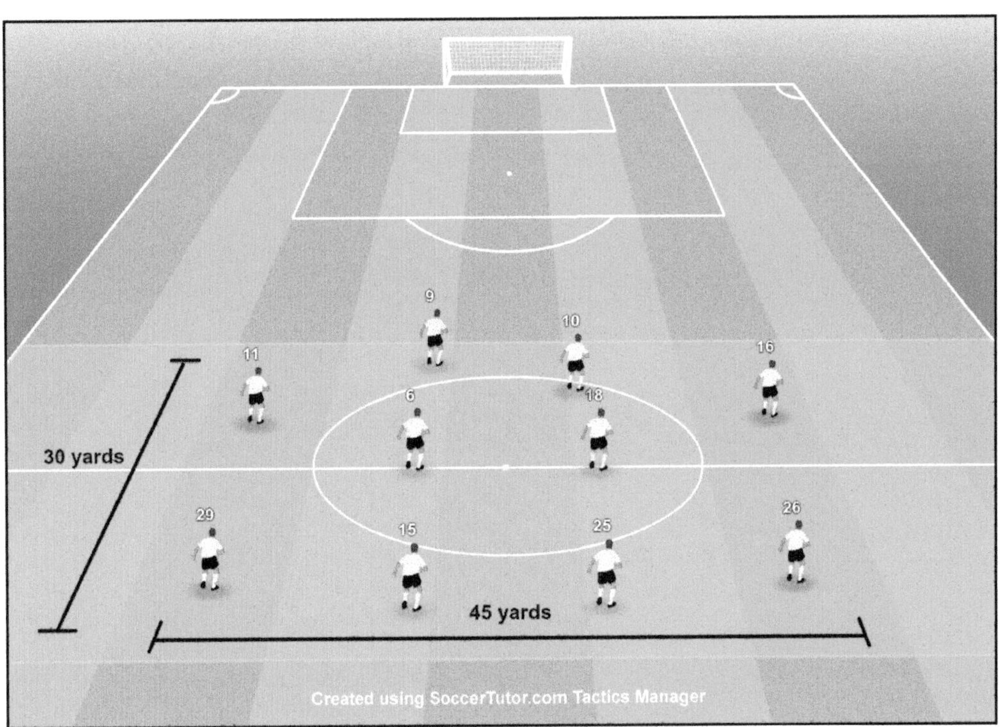

When defending within the middle third, the players created a compact formation (30 x 45 yards). This reduced the available space for the opponents between the lines and enabled the players to cover for each other as they retained short distances between each player within the line.

DEFENDING TACTICAL SITUATION 5

Putting Pressure on Midfielders Positioned Between the Lines

Putting Pressure On Midfielders Positioned Between The Lines

One of the main aims for the midfielders when defending within the middle third was to prevent the opposition players from receiving a pass in between the lines (forwards and midfielders) and turn towards their goal. In order to prevent this happening, they tried to keep the team compact and apply extremely high pressure when the ball was directed towards the opposition players.

Situation 1

The ball is in the centre back's (4) possession. No.9 moves to apply pressure, but not in an aggressive way. No.10 shifts towards the inside and the other midfielders (except for the winger on the strong side) shift towards the strong side and maintain the line's cohesion.

The distance between the forwards and the midfielders is kept small so there is not much space available (blue marked zone) for the opposition players.

Red No.4 passes to No.6 and Kehl (5) takes advantage of the transmission phase to put pressure on the new player in possession. The short distance between him and No.6 helps to achieve his main aim which is to prevent the No.6 from turning with the ball towards Borussia Dortmund's goal.

The other midfielders (11 and 8) create a defensive triangle while No.9 and No.10 move towards the ball area to take advantage of a potential interception. No.17 stays in an advanced position which enables him to control No.3, but mainly allows him to move quickly forward for the positive transition.

Situation 2

Red No.4 passes the ball towards the sideline and to the right back No.2.

Reus (11) takes advantage of the transmission phase and puts pressure on the man in possession.

Kehl (5) drops into a supporting position and Lewandowski (9) together with Mkhitaryan (10) also drops back to keep the distance between the midfielders and the forwards short and reduce the space for the opposition midfielders.

Red No.2 passes to No.6 who is positioned between Borussia Dortmund's midfield and defensive lines.

Kehl moves immediately to close the man in possession down and Lewandowski together with Mkhitaryan, move close to the ball area to take advantage of a potential interception. Reus (11) and Sahin (18) create a defensive triangle. Aubameyang (17) is in an advanced position.

Situation 3

This is a similar situation to the previous one.

The difference this time is that Mkhitaryan (10) is in a deeper position and close to the strong side.

Red No.4 passes the ball towards the sideline and to the red right back No.2.

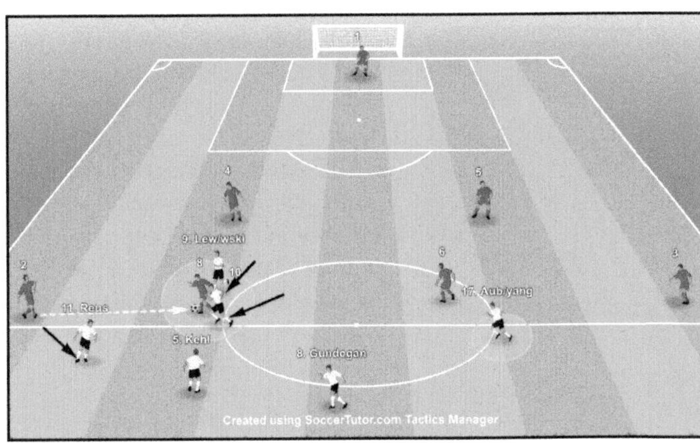

After receiving, No.2 passes to No.6 and as Mkhitaryan (10) is close to him he takes over the role of the first defender while Kehl (5) stays in a deep position.

Lewandowski (9) also drops back a few yards and gets ready to help double mark red No.6 or take advantage of Mkhitaryan's potential intervention. Aubameyang (17) is in an advanced position.

Situation 4

In this situation there is a through pass from red No.4 towards No.8.

Aubameyang (17) moves to put pressure on No.8 from behind while Gundogan (8) moves to contest him from the front.

It is very likely that red No.8 will be dispossessed if he decides to try and turn.

Situation 5

In this situation the red team manage to direct the ball to No.8 after two consecutive passes.

No.6 receives and is facing Borussia Dortmund's goal. Gundogan (8) was unable to close him down on time due to the quick passing combination.

As the main aim of Dortmund's midfielders (to prevent the midfielder from receiving and turning) has not been achieved, the players drop back to get more compact. With this reaction the players retain a safety distance and the available passing lanes become narrower. It is difficult for the player in possession to make a successful vertical or diagonal through pass.

As soon as the midfielders manage to get compact, the closest player to the man in possession moves to close him down.

The aim is to force the player in possession (6) to make a horizontal pass or a pass back.

Tactical Analysis: Pressing Midfielders Who Move To Receive In Free Space Near The Sideline

If one of the opposition midfielders shifted towards the sideline to receive within the free space, Borussia Dortmund triggered special mechanisms to deal with the situation.

Situation 1

Red No.8 moves towards the sideline to receive within the free space (blue zone shown in diagram).

Borussia Dortmund's defensive midfielder (5) does not follow his movement, so that he is able to help retain the midfield line with good shape and balance.

As No.8 has moved into Reus's zone of responsibility and receives the pass from No.4, Reus (11) is the player who moves to close him.

As there is already a player inside his zone of control (red No.2) his main aim is to prevent No.8 from turning with the ball and passing towards No.2. Lewandowski (9) drops back near the ball area to help double mark red No.8 and Kehl (5) shifts into a supporting position.

Situation 2

If the distance between the opposition midfielder No.8 and the winger (Reus) is far enough and Reus realises that he is unable to close him down in time to prevent him from turning, the best option was to stay focused on the full back (2) within his zone of responsibility.

The player who takes over the role of contesting red No.8 is the centre forward (9) while the other Dortmund midfielders drop back to retain a safety distance.

Session For This Tactical Situation *(5 Practices)*

1. Pressing Midfielders Positioned Between the Lines and Retaining a Compact Formation

Objective

Retaining a compact formation and limiting the available space for the opposition midfielders.

Description

This is a simple practice within a 50 x 50 yard area. There are two centre backs positioned on the blue cones (red No.4 and No.5).

The practice starts as soon as one of the red centre backs moves forward with the ball. The closest yellow player (No.9 in diagram) takes up a defensive position and the rest of the players adjust their positioning, making sure to retain short distances, keep a straight line and maintain a good defensive shape. When the man in possession stops his forward movement the yellow players also stop. When the player in possession passes back, the yellow players move forward all together as a compact unit.

Coaching Points

1. The key in this practice is for all the yellow players to constantly retain a compact formation.
2. Players need to have quick responses to the changing situation, depending on the red player's action.

PROGRESSION

2. Applying Immediate Pressure on Midfielders (Prevent Them From Turning) in a Dynamic Zonal Practice

Objective

Applying immediate pressure on the opposition midfielders to prevent them from turning.

Description

This is a high tempo practice. There is a 45 x 8 yard zone as shown in the diagrams. The 4 red defenders are positioned on the blue cones and the red midfielders (6 and 8) move freely within the light blue central zone.

The coach starts the practice by passing to one of the centre backs and the reds pass the ball around. The yellow players must take up positions according to the position of the ball, retaining good shape and cohesion.

The reds aim is to pass into one of the mini goals, either by a full back's pass (from the blue cones within the dark blue zone) or by a midfielder receiving within the light blue zone, turning and passing into a mini goal.

The yellow players try to prevent the reds from achieving their aims by immediately applying pressure on the man in possession and by creating defensive triangles to provide cover in case the red player decides to beat his direct opponent. The coach keeps passing new balls inside to keep the tempo high.

Restrictions

1. The full backs must score from within the dark blue zones and the midfielders can score from anywhere, but they must receive within the light blue central zone.
2. When the coach passes a new ball into play, there should be at least one pass played between the defenders before they try to score. Passes between the midfielders are not allowed.
3. The yellow players should only enter the blue zone after the pass towards the player within their zone of responsibility has being made.

Coaching Points

1. The yellow players need to constantly retain a compact formation.
2. The practice should be played at a high tempo throughout.
3. Players need to react quickly to take advantage of the transmission phase.
4. Communication between the players is important to retain short distances and collectively react to the changing situation.

PROGRESSION

3.Applying Immediate Pressure on Midfielders (Prevent Them From Turning) in a Dynamic Zonal Practice (2)

Description

This is a progression of the previous practice. We add two forwards for the yellow team.

The forwards defend in a passive way (they do not try to block the through passes), but when the ball is directed towards the full backs (2 and 3) or the midfielders (6 or 8) they move to help their teammates (as shown in the diagrams).

The reds try to score in the 3 mini goals and the yellows try to prevent them. During the first phase (e.g. 3 minutes) the yellows only try to stop their opponents from scoring. After this period they try to win possession and then finish their counter attack within 8-10 seconds.

The goalkeeper passes a new ball into play every time a goal is scored or the ball goes out of play.

Restrictions

1. The full backs must score from within the dark blue zones and the midfielders can score from anywhere, but they must receive within the light blue central zone.
2. When the goalkeeper passes a new ball into play, there should be at least one pass played between the defenders before they try to score. The red midfielders are allowed to pass to each other in this progression.
3. The yellow players should only enter the blue zone after the pass towards the player within their zone of responsibility has being made.

PROGRESSION

4. Pressing Midfielders and Retaining a Compact Formation in a Zonal Dynamic 9 v 9 Small Sided Game

Description

This progression is a competitive 9 v 9 game between two teams. The team in possession (red in diagram) try to find a way to pass the ball towards the forwards within the low white zone. As soon as this happens, the forwards (red 9 and 10) play against the strong side's defender (No.15 in diagram) who enters the playing area. If the yellow players win possession, they must then finish their counter within 8-10 seconds. After five attempts the teams switch roles.

Restrictions

1. The full backs must pass forward from within the dark blue zones and the midfielders can pass forward from anywhere, but they must receive within the light blue central zone.
2. The forwards of the defending team (yellows) are not allowed to enter the high white zone to put pressure on the centre backs. However, if the defender with the ball moves out of it they can then contest him.
3. The defender on the strong side can close the forward down only after the pass has been made.

PROGRESSION

5. Pressing Midfielders and Retaining a Compact Formation in a 7 Zone Dynamic 8 v 9 Small Sided Game

Description

The two teams play a 8 v 9 game in 2/3 of a full pitch. The red goalkeeper's starts and passes to one of his defenders. The red team try to find a way to pass to the forwards (9 and 10) inside the low white zone. The pass can be from the midfielders after receiving within the light blue central zone or from the full backs within one of the dark blue zones. As soon as this takes place there is a 2 v 1 situation that the forwards try to take advantage of within the white zone, in order to score. The yellows try to prevent the reds from achieving their aims, win the ball and then finish their counter attack within 8-10 seconds.

Restriction

The forwards of the defending team (yellows) are not allowed to enter the high yellow zone to put pressure on the centre backs, unless the defender with the ball moves out of it.

Coaching Points

1. The four coaching points from practice 2 apply again here.
2. Quick combination play is needed in the final third, as well as accurate finishing.

DEFENDING TACTICAL SITUATION 6

Preventing Through Balls

Preventing Through Balls

Another one of the main aims for Borussia Dortmund's midfielders was to prevent the through passes towards the opposition players positioned behind them. This would enable the defenders to stay close to each other without being forced to step forward (closer to the opponents who were positioned between the lines) and therefore create gaps in the defensive line. In order to block the passing lanes, the Dortmund midfielders defended the space.

Even if there were five opponents between the lines (midfield and defensive lines) creating a 5 v 4 situation, the Dortmund midfielders defended the space rather than moving into deeper positions. This gave the team an advantage when counter attacking if they managed to block a through pass because they could attack, leaving many opposition players behind them.

Situation 1

In order for Dortmund's forwards and midfielders to prevent through passes towards the opposition forwards, they had to retain a safe distance between them. The longer the distance between the defender in possession and the midfielders, the more time the midfielders had to react to a pass.

However, as it has already been mentioned, the Dortmund players tried to keep a compact formation so that the defenders were 30 yards away from the forwards. The distance between the forwards and the midfielders had to be kept at no more than 15 yards.

This distance enabled the midfielders to keep the space between them and the forwards limited for the opponent midfielders, as well as to allow enough time to react to a potential through pass from the defenders. In the situation above, red No.5 receives the pass from No.4 and before Mkhitaryan (10) manages to close him down, he has available time to make a forward through pass.

Aubameyang (17) stays in a central position in order to block the vertical pass. However, he should not shift towards the centre extensively as he also has to control the full back (3).

Gundogan (8) shifts towards the right to narrow the available vertical passing lane. As shown in the diagram, the distance from Aubameyang and Gundogan to red No.5 gives them enough time to react after the pass is made. This means that the passing lane can become even narrower and almost impossible to make a successful through pass.

The positioning of Aubameyang (17) enables him to take advantage of the transmission phase and intercept the through pass of No.5.

If No.5's pass is directed towards the full back instead, Aubameyang (17) can also take advantage of the transmission phase and catch No.3 before he manages to move further forward.

Situation 2

If the defender in possession moved forward with the ball, the Borussia Dortmund midfielders had to adjust their positioning. Specifically in this situation shown in the diagram, No.5 receives and has available time and space before Mkhitaryan (10) manages to close him down, so he moves forward. This reaction reduces the distance to the Dortmund midfielders so their reaction time is reduced too. The final result of this forward movement is that a successful through pass is more likely than before, despite the fact that the distance between the Gundogan (8) and Aubameyang (17) stays the same.

The reaction of the midfielders to the situation is to drop back to retain a safety distance which will result in a narrower passing lane, together with maintaining the correct team shape.

Furthermore, by dropping back they allow Mkhitaryan (10) time to close the player in possession down. The team then becomes compact again and the danger of a through ball has been dealt with.

Situation 3

If an opposition midfielder managed to receive facing Borussia Dortmund's goal and the Dortmund midfielders were not as compact as they should be, they had to be aware of the positioning of the opposition forwards.

Red No.6 moves forward after receiving and Lewandowski (9) tracks his run. The defensive midfielders Kehl and Gundogan (8) who are several yards apart, drop back to prevent a potential pass to the two opposition forwards (Red 9 and 10) until Lewandowski closes No.6 down or they manage to create a compact formation.

Session For This Tactical Situation *(4 Practices)*

1. Preventing Through Balls With a Compact and Cohesive Midfield Line

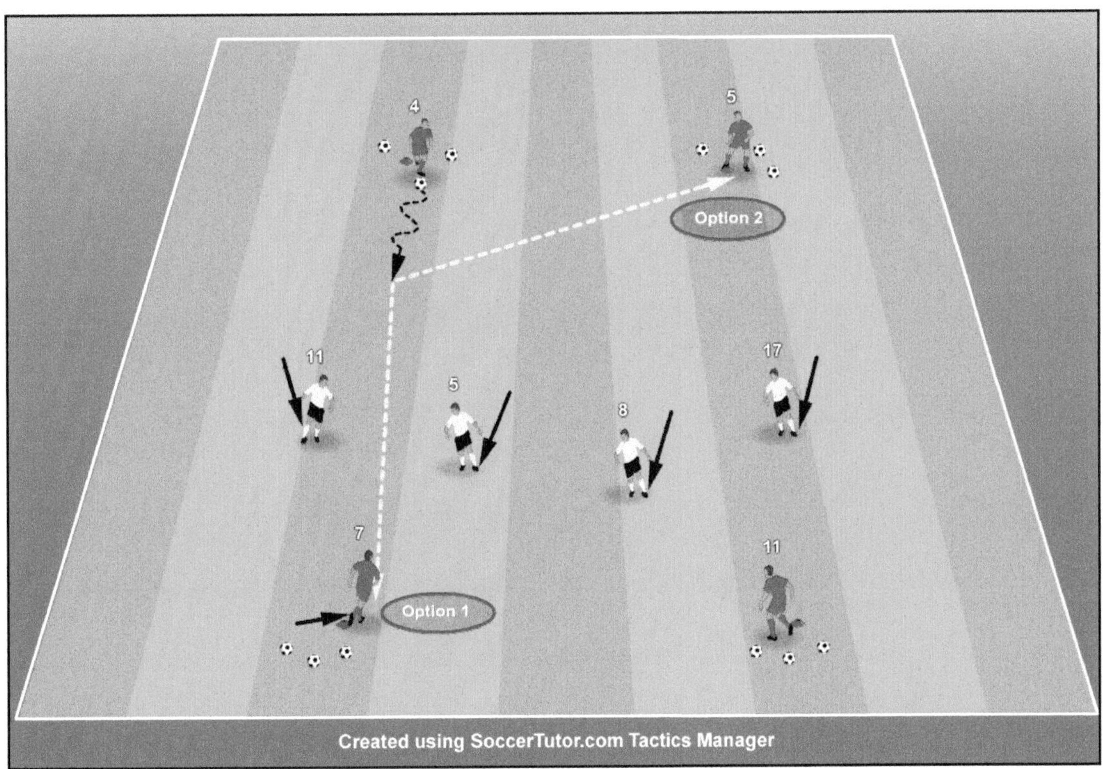

Objective

Retaining a 'safety distance' and preventing the opposition centre backs from playing through balls.

Description

In a 50 x 50 yard area, there are two red players on each side (on the blue cones as shown) and four yellow midfielders in the middle.

The red player in possession (No.4 in diagram) moves forward with the ball and either tries to make a through ball between the midfielders (option 1) or passes back to the other centre back (option 2).

The yellow players have to adjust their positioning in order to retain the appropriate shape and maintain a safety distance (15-18 yards). If a through pass (option 1) is attempted, the yellow midfielders try to intercept the ball. If the centre back passes back, the yellow midfielders move forward to retain the same safety distance (15-18 yards). If the ball is passed to a red player on the other side, they then have the same aim in the opposite direction. The red team score 1 point for every successful through ball. The players switch positions after 2 minutes.

PROGRESSION

2. Pressing Centre Backs, Preventing Through Balls and Forcing the Ball Wide

Objective

Preventing the opposition centre backs from playing through balls and controlling the full backs.

Description

In the same 50 x 50 yard area, to make this practice more realistic and to make sure the wingers do not stay too central, two red full backs are added. The two red centre backs inside the light blue zone (4 and 5) pass the ball to each other while the forwards and the midfielders of the yellow team take up positions according to the position of the ball.

The red centre backs can either pass from within the zone or move into the main area. They can make a through pass towards the forwards inside the dark blue zone (option 1) or pass towards a full back (option 2). They can also pass back again, waiting for the forwards to be unbalanced before taking advantage of free space to pass forward. The yellow players try to prevent the through balls and control the full backs in order to catch them before they dribble the ball through the cone gates.

Restriction

The forwards are only allowed to contest the defenders after they move out of the light blue zone.

PROGRESSION

3. Pressing Centre Backs, Preventing Through Balls and Forcing the Ball Wide in a 6 Zone Dynamic Practice

Description

In this progression, two red midfielders (6 and 8) and two central zones are added. The reds team still have the same two aims they had in the previous practice, but now also have a third aim to move the ball to the midfielders inside the white zone, either directly from the centre backs or through the full backs as shown in the diagram.

The yellow midfielders are positioned outside the red zone with a long distance between them and the red midfielders (6 and 8). This enables the red midfielders to receive and turn with the ball. The 4 yellow midfielders have to read the tactical situation and drop back to prevent a through pass between them. This gives the forwards time to close the man in possession down or if this is not possible, as soon as they are compact the closest player moves forward and closes him down (as shown in diagram).

The reds score if they pass to the forwards (7 or 11) or if the full back manages to dribble through the cone gate. If the yellows win possession, they must finish their counter attack within 8-10 seconds.

Restrictions

1. The forwards can only move to contest the red defenders once they move outside the light blue zone.
2. The yellow forwards can only enter the white zone after the pass.
3. The yellow midfielders can only enter the red zone after the pass towards a red midfielder.
4. The full backs can only score if the ball is passed to them by the centre backs.

VARIATION

4. Pressing Centre Backs, Preventing Through Balls and Forcing the Ball Wide in a 6 Zone Dynamic Practice (2)

Objective

Preventing through balls when there is no cohesion in midfield.

Description

In this variation of the previous practice, the only aim for the reds is to move the ball either directly or through the full backs to the midfielders inside the white zone and then play a successful through ball to the forwards in the dark blue zone. This time the starting positions of the two yellow wingers is inside the purple zones near the sidelines.

As soon as the ball reaches a red midfielder, the two yellow defensive midfielders (5 and 8) drop back and take up positions to block the passing lanes to the two red forwards. This gives time for the wingers to converge and prevent the through balls and for the yellow forwards to close the man in possession down. If the yellows win possession, they must finish their counter attack within 8-10 seconds.

Coaching Points

1. Players need to take up their positions while being aware of the positions of the forwards.
2. There needs to be good communication between the players to retain cohesion in their movements.

DEFENDING TACTICAL SITUATION 7

The Defenders' Reaction to Through Balls

The Defenders' Reaction To Through Balls

As we have already explained, the defenders tried to retain the cohesion of the line during the defensive phase by maintaining short distances between the players. Their main aims were to avoid creating space (gaps within the line) for the opposition forwards to exploit and to prevent the opposition players who were positioned between the lines from turning with the ball when they received through passes.

In order to achieve both aims the defenders left their positions and moved into more advanced ones, but only in cases when it was absolutely necessary. When they moved out of position, they did not move into very advanced positions directly. Instead they moved only a few yards forward to reduce the distance from their direct opponent and waited for the pass to be made in order to move further forward to then apply pressure. This meant they retained a position which enabled them to drop back again and provide help to their teammates if their direct opponent did not receive a pass.

Situation 1

Red No.6 receives the pass between the lines and is able to pass forward. Red No.9 moves to provide a passing option.

As the passing lane is very narrow and it is unlikely No.9 will receive a pass, the Borussia Dortmund centre back Subotic (4) does not follow him, but instead stays together with his teammates.

Situation 2

This time the passing lane towards No.9 is wider and he is very likely to receive a pass.

Subotic (4) moves a few yards forward to be close (but not very close) to his direct opponent in order to prevent him from turning if the ball is directed to him. This reaction from Subotic creates space in behind him, but he is still close to his teammates.

Red No.6 passes to No.9 and as soon as the ball leaves No.6's foot, Subotic (4) moves to take advantage of the transmission phase and put him under pressure in order to prevent him turning with the ball.

The other defenders shift inside to create a defensive triangle to provide cover. The defensive midfielders (8 and 5) move close to the ball area to apply double or triple marking. The man in possession is forced to move or pass backwards.

If the pass is directed to No.10 instead who exploits the free space in behind No.4, Hummels (15) tracks his run and because Subotic (4) is not in an advanced position, this enables him to drop back immediately and provide support to Hummels in case of a lost duel.

Situation 3

If the forward (9) moves towards an available passing lane, but he drops very deep near to the Dortmund defensive midfielders, his direct marker moves a few yards forward to control him (but he does not go too deep).

As soon as the ball is passed to the forward (9), the Borussia Dortmund midfielders take advantage of the transmission phase and drop back in order to catch him (mainly Kehl).

The defenders also drop back and converge to block the passing lanes, allowing the midfielders time to take over the job of contesting the man in possession.

Session For This Tactical Situation *(4 Practices)*

1. Defending Passes to the Forwards: Decision Making and Cohesive Reactions

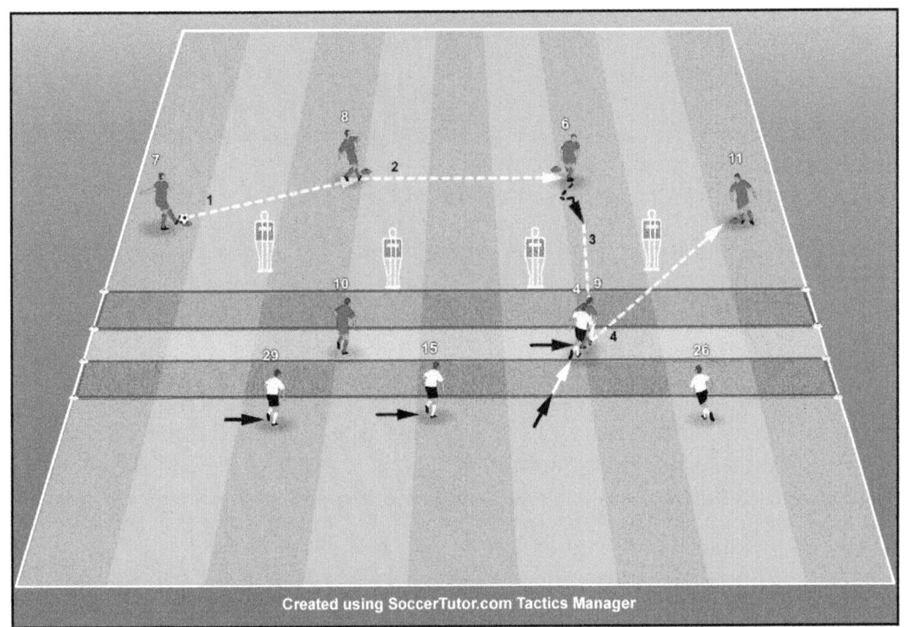

Objective

To develop defenders' reactions and cohesive movements to prevent through balls.

Description

In a 45 x 45 yard area, the red midfielders (6, 7, 8 and 9) are positioned on the blue cones and start the practice by passing the ball to each other. The yellow defenders take up positions according to the position of the ball. There are also two red forwards (9 and 10) who move within the middle white zone.

If the midfielder in possession decides to move forward with the ball he is free to pass forward. If one of the forwards takes up a position towards a passing lane, his direct marker has to enter the red zone to reduce his distance from him. If the midfielder decides to pass back, the yellow defender returns to his starting position outside the red zone (diagram 1).

If the ball is passed to the forward, the defender takes advantage of the transmission phase to move further forward and contest him in order to prevent him from turning (diagram 2). If the forward decides to pass back instead of turning, the defender moves back to his starting position and drops further back together with his teammates to give time for the imaginary midfielders to close the man in possession down (diagram 3).

Coaching Points

1. Players need to read the specific tactical situation with good communication between them.
2. Quick reactions needed to take advantage of the transmission phase (time the ball takes to travel).

PROGRESSION

2. Preventing Through Balls by Using 'Controlling Positions' and Providing Cover in Defence

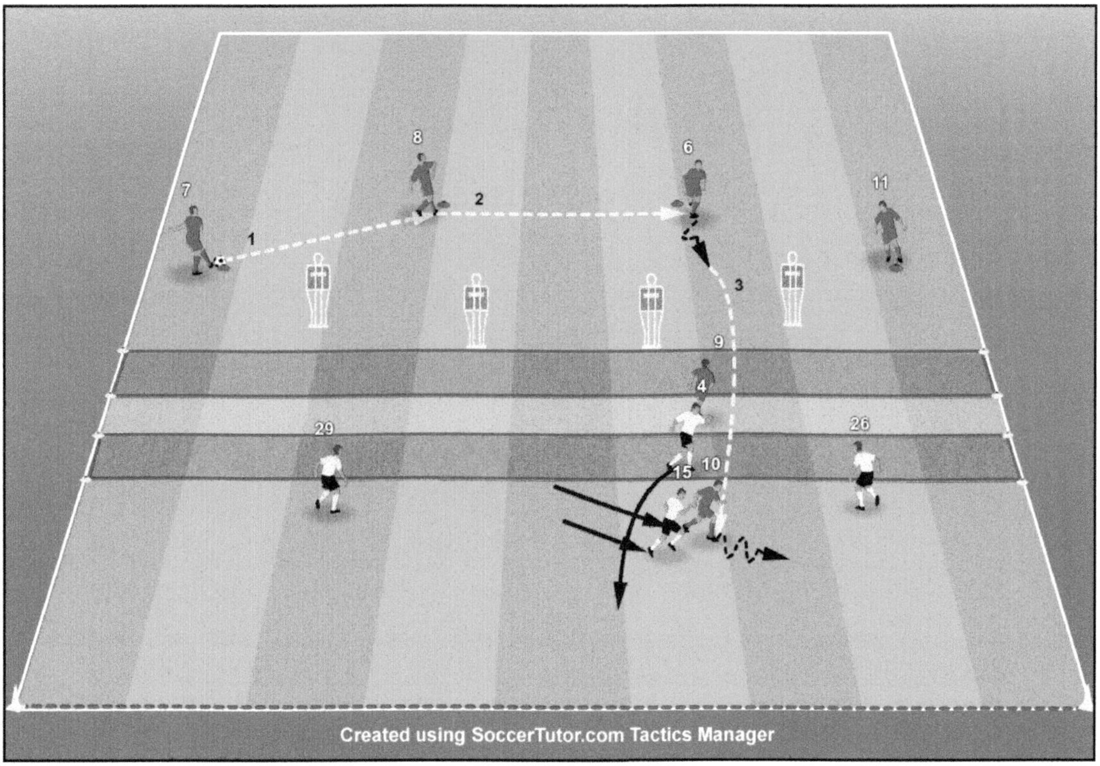

Objective

To prevent through balls by using 'controlling' positions and providing cover in defence.

Description

This is a variation of the previous practice. The focus this time is on how important it is not to move too high up the pitch, but instead to remain in a controlling position (inside the red zone) so the defender is able to provide cover immediately after the long ball towards the available space.

The practice starts with the red midfielders in possession as they pass the ball to each other. Once one of them decides to move forward, one of the forwards (No.9) moves towards the most obvious passing lane and the other one (No.10) tries to take advantage of the space behind him and receive the long ball. The defender who has entered the red zone (No.4 in diagram) must drop back quickly and provide cover for his teammate No.15, to prevent No.10 from dribbling the ball through the end line.

Restriction

Only the advanced defender (No.4 in diagram) can provide cover and help his teammate.

PROGRESSION

3. Preventing Through Balls with Good Decision Making and Cohesive Movement in a Dynamic 8 v 7 SSG

Description

In this progression, one red forward, four yellow midfielders and a goalkeeper are added. The coach starts and passes to a red midfielder. The yellow midfielders do not move forward to put pressure on them, but instead retain their shape and defend passively without trying to stop the potential through passes. The red forwards (7, 9 and 10) move within the three zones and try to receive a pass. According to which zone the ball is received in by the red forward, the yellow defenders react in 3 ways:

WHITE ZONE: 1) The forward in possession is put under pressure once the ball is passed to him in order to prevent him from turning. 2) Instead of passing to the forward inside the white zone, the ball is directed towards the created space so the players move to provide cover (especially the advanced defender).

BLUE ZONE: 3) The defenders drop back. The midfielders move to contest the man in possession.

The reds aim to score a goal against the goalkeeper and the yellows try to prevent them from scoring, win the ball and find a way to pass it to the coach inside the light blue zone within 6-8 seconds.

Restrictions

1. The yellow midfielders can track back and enter the middle zones as soon as the pass is made.
2. If the yellows win possession, there are no longer any restrictions in regards to the zones.

PROGRESSION

4. Preventing Through Balls With Good Decision Making and Cohesive Movement in a Dynamic 9 v 8 (+GK) SSG

Description

In this progression we play a 9 v 8 (+GK) game in 2/3 of a full sized pitch. The coach starts the practice by passing to one of the red players in the low zone, where we have a 5 v 4 situation.

The red players (2, 3, 5, 6 and 8) in the low zone try to find a way to make a through pass towards one of the four forwards (7, 9, 10 and 11). At the same time, the yellow midfielders (5, 8, 11 and 17) defend in a passive way and leave the through passes unblocked.

The yellow defenders (15, 4, 26 and 29) have to read the tactical situation and react accordingly. After the through pass is made, the yellow midfielders switch to active defending and try to prevent the red players from scoring, together with the yellow defenders.

If the yellows win possession, they must then try to score in the mini goals within 8-10 seconds. After the first 5 minutes, the yellow midfielders defend actively in both phases of the game.

DEFENDING TACTICAL SITUATION 8

Defending Near the Sideline

Defending Near The Sideline

The wingers worked in collaboration with the full backs in situations when the opposition full backs made runs into advanced positions. Borussia Dortmund's players tried to deal with these runs by defending the space and switching who they were marking, rather than following their direct opponents away from their zones of responsibility.

This enabled the Borussia Dortmund players to retain balanced positions which enabled them to move forward quickly and counter attack against an unbalanced team in case possession was won.

Situation 1 - The Opposition Full Back is in an Advanced Position

As the ball is in the centre back's possession, Reus (11) is positioned towards the centre to block a potential vertical pass. Depending on the opposition full back's (2) position, Reus can take up a position:

a. Deeper than the full back
b. In line with the full back
c. A few yards higher (shown in diagram).

This positioning of Reus may look risky, but it enables him to provide safety and have an effective counter attacking position if possession is won (as the red full back No.2 will be left behind).

As soon as the pass is made towards the full back (2), Reus takes advantage of the transmission phase (the time when the ball is travelling) and closes No.2 down before he manages to move further forward.

The other Dortmund midfielders and forwards drop back to retain a good shape and compactness.

Situation 2 - Double Marking the Opposition Winger

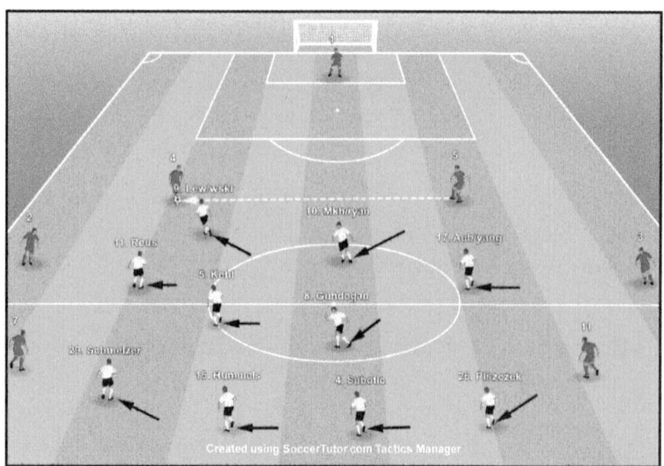

In this situation, Reus (11) takes up a deeper position in regards to the positioning of the red right back No.2.

The ball is passed from one red centre back to the other and all of Borussia Dortmund's players shift according to the position of the ball.

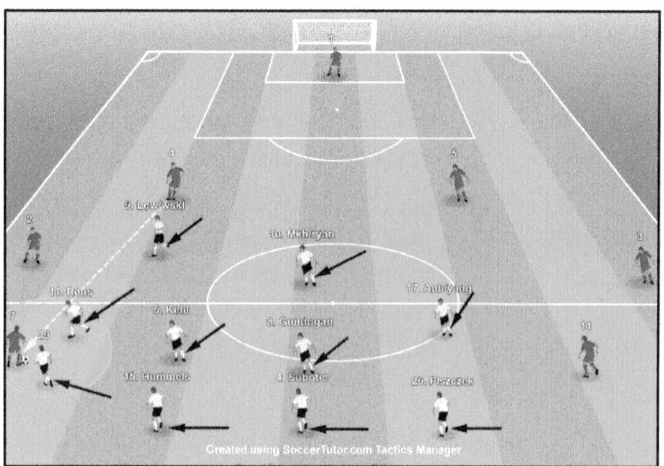

As soon as the ball leaves No.4's foot, the left back Schmelzer (29) and the left winger Reus (11) take advantage of the transmission phase and both put pressure on the new man in possession (red No.7 - the right winger near the sideline).

While double marking is applied, the other players shift to retain a good shape and compactness.

Tactical Analysis: Defending The Forward Run Of The Full Back On The Strong Side

If one of the opposition midfielders shifted towards the sideline to receive within the free space, Borussia Dortmund triggered special mechanisms to deal with the situation.

Situation 1

When the opposition full back on the strong side made a forward run to receive in an advanced position, Dortmund's players (full back and winger) defended the space rather than tracking their opponents within their zone of responsibility. However, certain mechanisms had to be triggered for the successful collaboration between the two. In this situation, the ball is passed to No.4 who has available space before Lewandowski (9) is able to close him down.

Red No.4 dribbles forward as there is an open ball situation and No.2 makes a forward run. At the same time, red No.7 drops back towards the potential passing lane. Reus (11) tracks No.2's forward run until he enters Piszczek's (26) zone of responsibility. If we assume that the distance between the defender and the midfielder is about 15 yards, then Reus has to track him for about half the distance (7-8 yards) and then leave him under the control of Piszczek (there must be a key word which triggers the switching in marking). A very important aspect for the successful collaboration of the two players is the blocking of the vertical pass. So as Reus drops back, he keeps (with the help of the defensive midfielder) the vertical passing lane very narrow. This makes it impossible for red No.7 to receive and allows Schmelzer (29) to stay focused on the full back (2).

Red No.4 passes to No.2 near the sideline, who is now under the control of Schmelzer (29).

The left winger Reus (11) drops back to help double mark No.2.

The defensive midfielder Kehl (5) takes over red No.7's marking. Borussia Dortmund can deal with the situation successfully without creating space on the flank for the opposition to exploit.

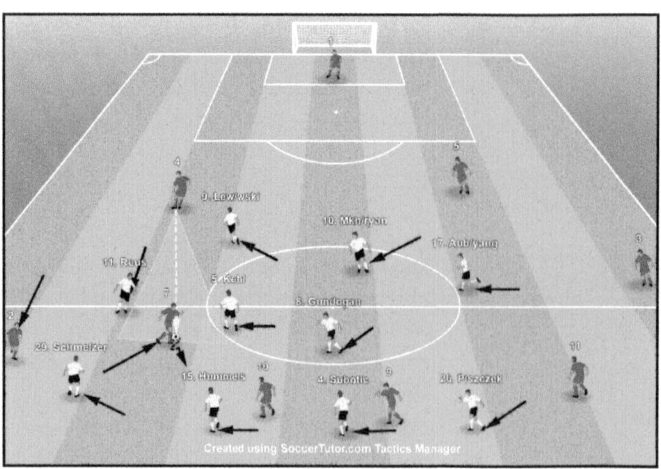

If the two players switch marking at the correct moment, but the vertical passing lane is not blocked, the opposition winger (7) can receive a through pass and move forward with the ball. He will then have many available passing options as there will be a 5 v 4 situation in favour of the reds.

Finally, if the two players (full back and winger) track their opponents rather than defend the zone, available space will be created for both the red full back (2) and the red No.10.

This space can be exploited by a long pass from No.4, as shown in the diagram.

Situation 2

The ball is passed to the red centre back No.4 who has available space before Lewandowski (9) can close him down.

Red No.4 dribbles forward and Lewandowski moves to close him down. As there is an open ball situation, the red right back (2) moves forward. The left winger Reus (11) tracks the run of red No.2 and the Dortmund left back Schmelzer (29) gets ready to take over the marking by shifting close to the sideline.

In addition, Reus (11) and the defensive midfielder Kehl (5) move to keep the vertical passing lane narrow.

Red No.2 has moved into Schmelzer's (29) zone of responsibility and Reus (11) has stopped tracking him. Instead, Schmelzer has taken over his marking.

The other players have shifted towards the strong side. Reus and Kehl (5) have made a pass towards red No.7 impossible by blocking the passing lane. The right winger Aubameyang (17) is in an advanced position and is ready to take part in a potential counter attack.

Situation 3

In this situation the red right winger (7) takes up an advanced position within Schmelzer's (29) zone of responsibility.

The red right back No.2 makes a forward run again and Reus (11) tracks him.

Reus stops tracking No.2 as he has entered Schmelzer's zone of responsibility. Red No.4 passes to the right back No.2 and Schmelzer (29) does not move to close the new player immediately as he has to pass on No.7's marking to a teammate. Instead, Schmelzer shifts into a position which enables him to control both red No.7 and No.2.

As soon as there is a switch in No.7's marking to No.15 Hummels (there may be a key word used during the players' communication), Schmelzer (29) moves to put pressure on the ball.

Session For This Tactical Situation *(4 Practices)*

1. Defending in Pairs Near the Sideline (Full Back and Winger)

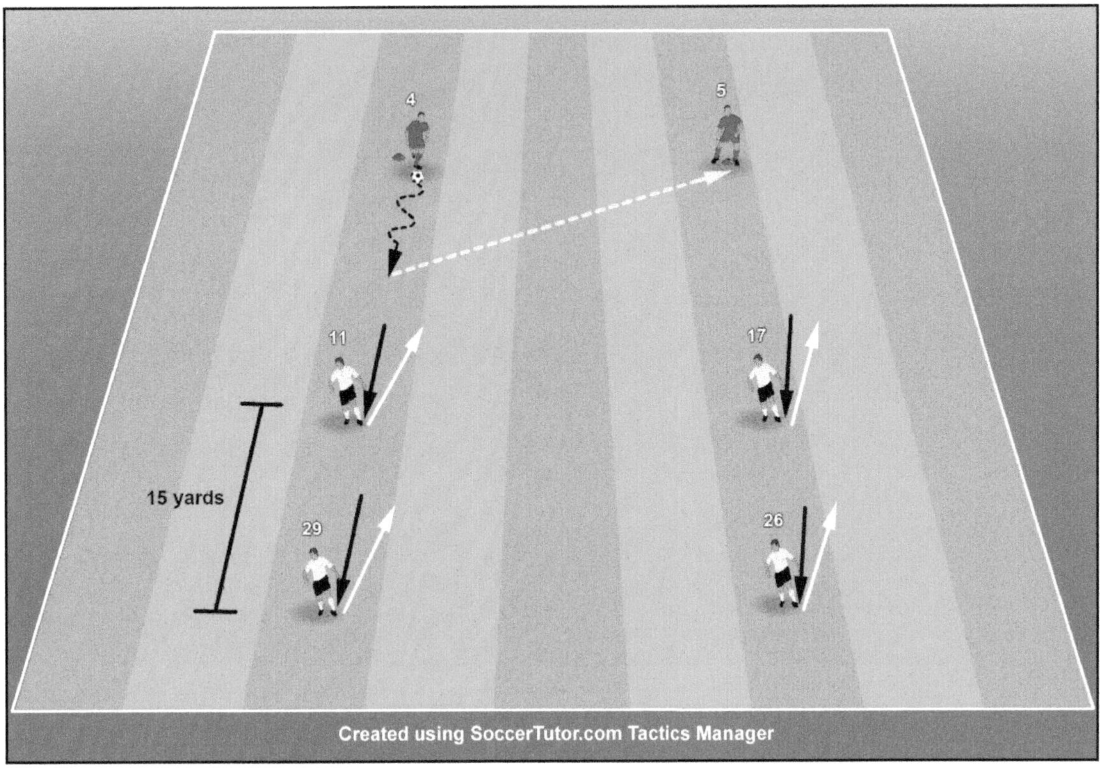

15 yards

Created using SoccerTutor.com Tactics Manager

Objective

The players (full back and winger) practice working in pairs to defend near the sideline.

Description

This is a simple practice played in a 45 x 45 yard area with the aim of getting the players used to retaining a stable distance between them (15 yards). The red centre backs are positioned on the blue cones while the yellow wingers and full backs work in pairs.

The players within the pair are positioned 15 yards apart from each other and 30 yards away from the other pair. The practice starts when one of the centre backs moves forward with the ball. The pairs try to retain a stable distance of 15 yards both from the man in possession and between them as well as 30 yards from the other pair. This means all the players need to work in synchronisation.

As soon as the man in possession passes to the other red centre back, the yellow players switch their orientation and move according to the new position of the ball.

PROGRESSION

2. Defending Near the Sideline in a 2 v 1 Situation

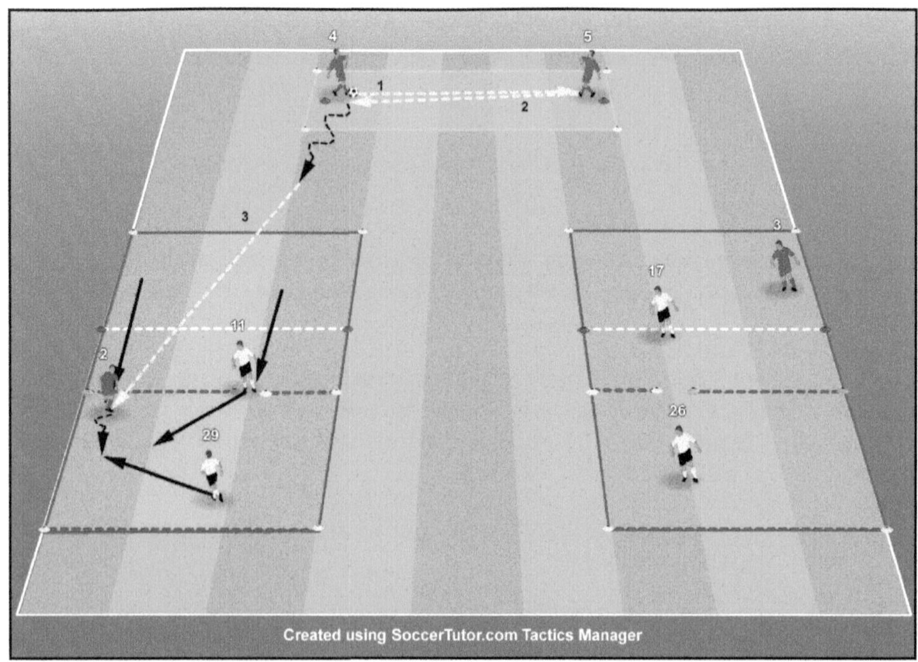

Description

In the same 45 x 45 yard area, there are two 25 x 15 yard zones. The two red centre backs pass to each other until one of them decides to move forward with the ball.

The red full back inside the zone on the strong side (No.2 in diagrams) tries to receive the ball within the high part of the zone (indicated by the red cones and white line) and dribble through the orange cone gate (diagram 1) or receive the ball beyond the orange cone gate and dribble through the red end line (diagram 2).

The reds score a point by dribbling through the yellow cone gate or the red end line. The centre back can score a point if he manages to pass through the orange cone gate successfully (diagram 2).

The yellow winger on the strong side (No.11 in diagram) must retain the correct distance from the full back so he can block a potential pass towards the orange cone gate and also control a pass towards the full back and contest him before he manages to dribble the ball through the orange cone gate (by taking advantage of the transmission phase) as shown in diagram 1.

If the full back receives beyond the orange cone gate, the winger moves to help double mark him together with the yellow full back (No.29 in diagrams) and prevent him from dribbling the ball through the red end line (diagram 2).

Restriction

The red full back should receive either deeper than the white line or beyond the orange cone gate.

Coaching Points

1. Players need to be able to read the tactical situation (react in the correct way depending on where the opposition full back is receiving the pass).
2. It is very important to take advantage of the transmission phase (the time the ball takes to travel to the full back) to close down the full back.
3. There needs to be good synchronisation between the yellow winger and full back, always maintaining the correct distances between them.
4. Communication between the players is key (the full back calls out a key word when the opposition full back enters his zone of responsibility).

PROGRESSION

3. Defending Near the Sideline in a 2 v 2 Situation

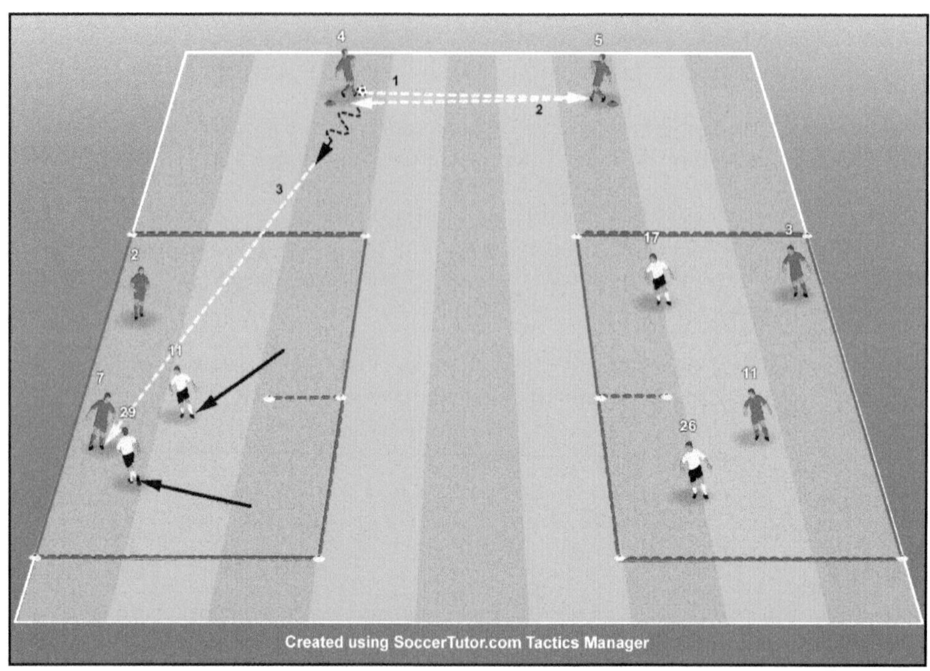

Description

In this progression of the previous practice, we add one red winger on each side. This time we just have one yellow cone gate near the middle of the zones towards the inside.

This time, the reds aims are as follows:

1. To dribble the ball through the red lines
2. Make a successful pass towards the yellow cone gate
3. Dribble the ball through the yellow cone gate

The yellows players try to prevent these aims by working in collaboration by applying double marking (diagram 1) or by switching the marking of the players at the appropriate moment and then double marking (diagram 2).

If the yellows players win possession, they try to dribble the ball through the end line on the other side.

Coaching Points

The coaching points from the previous practice apply again.

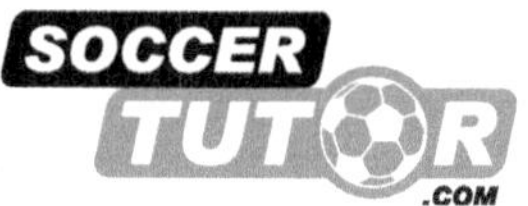

PROGRESSION

4. Defending Near the Sideline in a 9 v 9 Dynamic Small Sided Game With Side Zones

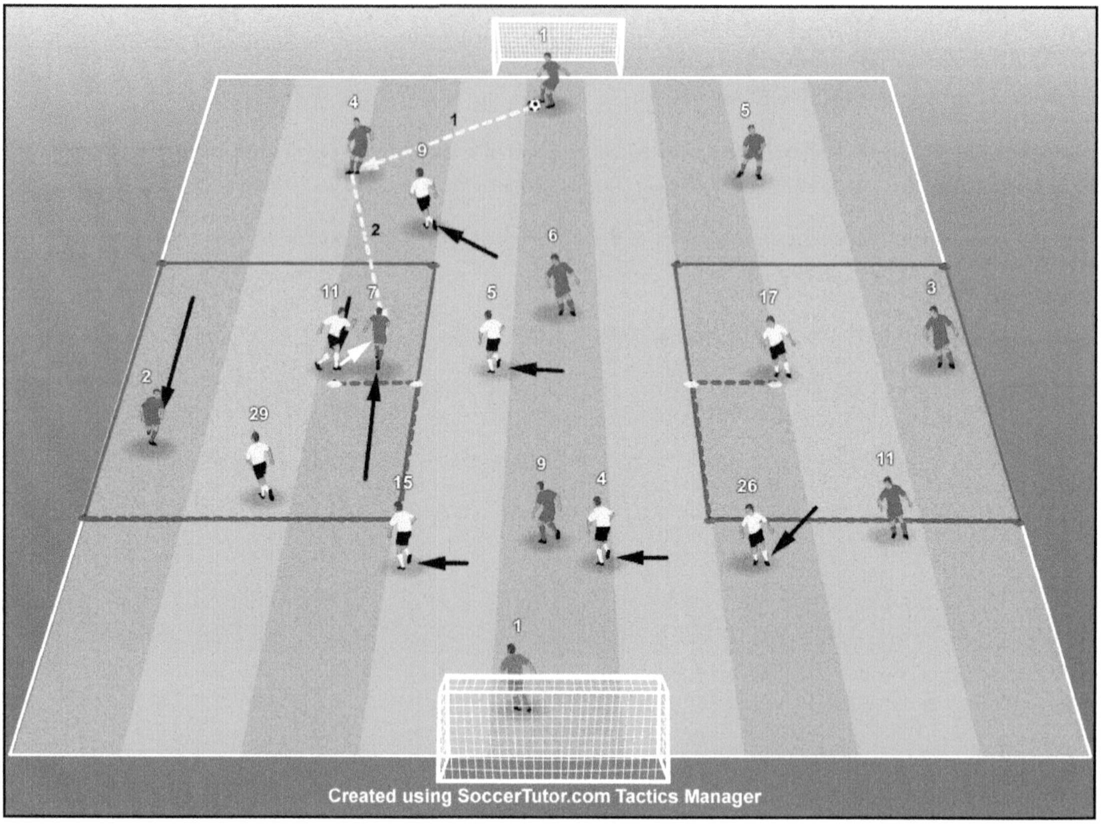
1
4
1
9
5
2
6
11
7
5
17
3
2
29
9
11
15
4
26
1
Created using SoccerTutor.com Tactics Manager

Description

In this final practice of the session, we play a 9 v 9 small sided game in a 55 x 45 yard area. The two teams play a normal game and both try to score.

The red team can also score in the following ways:

1. The centre back on the strong side manages to pass through the yellow cone gate
2. The full back and the winger manage to combine and one dribbles the ball through a red line
3. One of the players dribbles the ball through the yellow cone gate

If the ball goes out of play, the game starts again with the red goalkeeper in possession. If the yellows win possession, they must then finish their counter attack within 8-10 seconds.

DEFENDING TACTICAL SITUATION 9

Defending the Forward Run of the Full Back on the Weak Side

Defending The Forward Run Of The Full Back On The Weak Side

When the opposition were able to switch the point of attack towards the weak side and the opposition full back made a forward run, Borussia Dortmund's winger on the weak side tracked him. With this reaction, Borussia Dortmund managed to prevent the opposition from having too much time on the ball and at the same time, prevent them from creating a numerical advantage by bringing a defender into an advanced position.

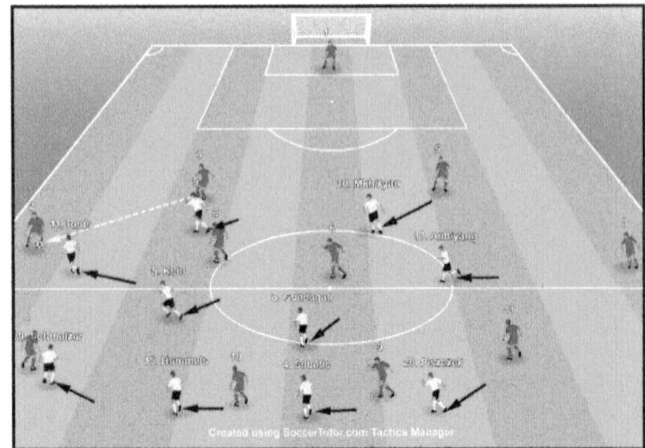

The ball is passed to red No.2 near the sideline and the Borussia Dortmund players shift towards the strong side.

The defenders maintain cohesion by staying close to each other.

The reds pass quickly to No.6 who has time before Gundogan (8) closes him down. The weak side's full back (3) makes a run to receive in an advanced position. Aubameyang (17) could not press No.6 and prevent him from passing, so he tracks No.3's run. When the defenders have shifted towards the left and kept short distances between each other, it is difficult for the weak side's full back to close No.3 quickly. So Aubameyang has to track No.3's run to deny him time and to prevent the reds from creating superiority in numbers.

Red No.6 plays a long pass to No.3 and Aubameyang (17) moves to close the receiver down. The defenders drop back and shift towards the strong side.

There are five red players moving forward. Aubameyang's reaction prevents the reds from creating a numerical advantage for their attack.

Tactical Analysis: Switching From Passive Defending To Pressing

When defending within the middle third there were times when Borussia Dortmund switched to pressing. This switch in the type of defending took place only if there were certain essential conditions and a certain trigger. Essential for switching from defending in a passive way to pressing was the positioning of the centre forward and the No.10 near the ball zone and towards the strong side.

The trigger was usually the centre forward's attempt to create a strong side and force the ball towards the sideline. As the vertical pass was blocked ,the ball was directed towards the full back. Then the winger moved very fast towards the full back in order to put him under pressure.

Situation 1 - Both the Centre Forward and No.10 are on the Strong Side

Red No.4 has the ball on Borussia Dortmund's left side. As the No.10 has a position which enables him to take up a position towards the strong side, he then signals Lewandowski (probably with a key word). Lewandowski (9) then moves to put pressure on the centre back in possession in a way which creates a strong side and forces the ball towards the sideline. This is the trigger for the rest of the players who get ready to switch to pressing.

As the vertical passing lane is blocked, No.4 is forced to pass to the right back No.2 near the sideline. As soon as the ball leaves No.4's foot, Reus (11) takes advantage of the transmission phase and moves quickly to put pressure on the new man in possession. Lewandowski (9) immediately blocks the back pass to red No.4 and No.10 marks red No.8 closely. The left back Schmelzer (29) also moves close to red No.7. All the potential passing options for the man in possession are now closely marked.

Situation 2 - Creating a Strong Side

Red No.5 passes to the other centre back No.4. The ball is directed to the side where the No.10 is positioned (in a deep position).

Instead of the No.10 moving forward to put pressure on No.4, the centre forward Lewandowski (9) moves to put pressure on him. This action forces the ball towards the side where the No.10 is positioned so there are good chances for Borussia Dortmund to create superiority in numbers near the ball area.

The quick shifting of Lewandowski towards the centre back is the trigger for the rest of the players.

As soon as the ball leaves red No.4's foot, the left winger Reus (11) takes advantage of the transmission phase and moves quickly to put pressure on the new man in possession (trigger).

At the same time, Lewandowski (9) blocks the back pass and Mkhitaryan (10) marks red No.6 from close distance.

Additionally, the left back Schmelzer (29) marks No.7 closely, so red No.2 has no available short passing options.

Session For This Tactical Situation *(4 Practices)*

1. Switching from Passive Defending to Pressing and Creating a Strong Side with a 3 v 2 Numerical Advantage

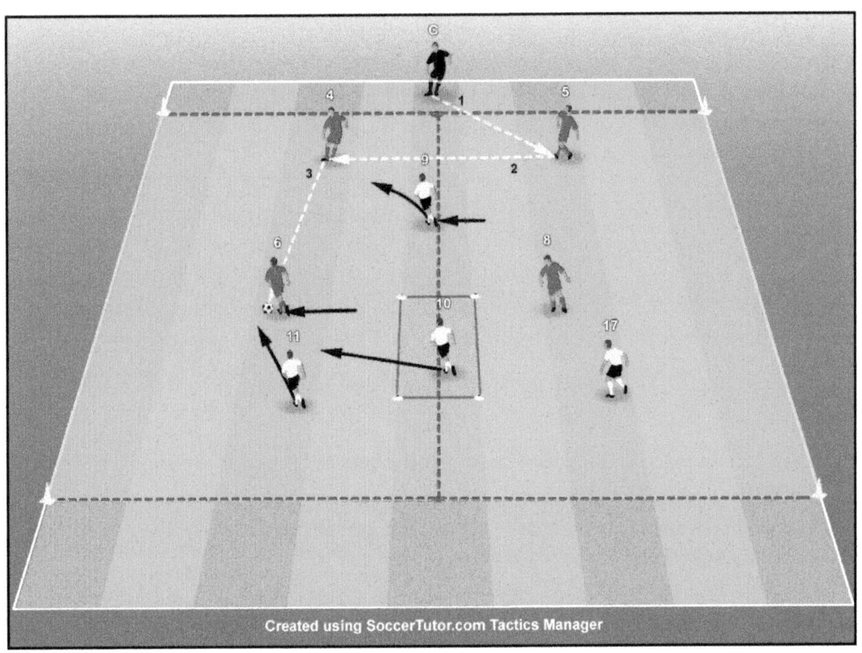

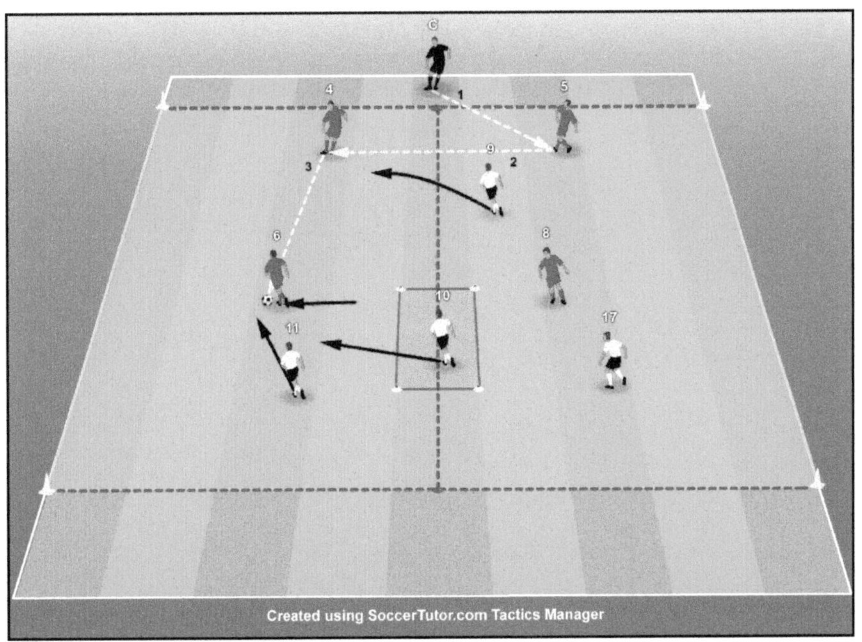

Objective

The players work on switching from passive defending to pressing.

Description

In a 30 x 20 yard area, we divide the pitch into two sides. The coach starts by passing to one of the red centre backs who pass the ball to each other. At the same time, No.9 shifts towards the left or right and defends in a passive way according to the position of the ball.

As soon as No.10 (who is positioned inside the dark blue central zone) calls out the key word, No.9 moves to put pressure on the ball and create a strong side (3 v 2 situation is created). The reds try to dribble the ball through the red end line or through the middle red line.

The yellows try to win possession and dribble the ball through the red end line on the strong side.

Variation

The centre forward (No.9) is the one who acts as the trigger by moving towards the centre back in a way which creates a strong side (diagram 2). No.10 and the other yellow players on the potential strong side must get ready to apply pressing and win possession.

Coaching Points

1. Players need to be able to read the tactical situation and recognise the trigger (when a strong side has been created by the centre forward's pressing).
2. The players must again take advantage of the transmission phase (they can use a key word as soon as the ball leaves the first centre back's foot so that No.9 has time to act).
3. There also needs to be good synchronisation in the defensive movements with the correct distances retained, as well as good communication.

PROGRESSION

2. Switching from Passive Defending to Pressing and Creating a Strong Side with a 4 v 3 Numerical Advantage

Description

In this progression of the previous practice, we add two players for each team within the 2 zones. There are also two more red players positioned outside of the zones, behind the red end line.

We add an extra aim for the red team. The red centre backs can now score a point by passing to the red outside players (No.9 and No.10), in addition to still scoring points by dribbling the ball through the red lines (middle and end).

The trigger was when the key word is called out by No.10 (diagram 1) or by No.9's attempt to create a strong side (diagram 2). This time the teams play 4 v 3 within the strong side of the pitch. The yellows try to win possession and dribble the ball through the red line on the other side.

Coaching Points

The coaching points from the previous practice apply again here.

PROGRESSION

3. Switching from Passive Defending to Pressing and Creating a Strong Side in a 2 Phase Dynamic SSG

Description

This practice is played in 2/3 of a full sized pitch and there are two phases. During the first phase ,the red defenders pass the ball around while the yellow players defend in a passive way and try to block the passes towards the two forwards inside the white zone.

As soon as there is a trigger, the practice moves on to the second phase and the yellows switch to pressing. They try to block the vertical pass of the centre back towards the forward and force the ball towards the full back. During the second phase, the reds can score with a successful through ball from the centre back towards the forward or by dribbling the ball through the red middle or end lines.

The yellow players try to prevent the reds from achieving their aims, win possession and then score within 8-10 seconds. When the yellows win possession there are no restrictions in regards to zones.

Restriction

Neither team is allowed to use long passes.

PROGRESSION

4. Switching from Passive Defending to Pressing and Creating a Strong Side in a Dynamic 11 v 11 Zonal Game

Description

In this progression, two teams play an 11 v 11 game. During the first phase, the yellow players defend in a passive way and try to block the passes towards the players inside the dark blue zone.

After a trigger, the game moves into the second phase and the yellows switch to pressing. They try to block the vertical pass of the centre back towards the forwards and force the ball wide. During the second phase, the reds can score by playing a through ball from the centre back to a forward inside the dark blue zone, dribbling the ball through the red middle line or scoring against the goalkeeper.

The yellow players try to prevent these aims, win possession and then score within 8-10 seconds. As soon as the yellows win possession, there are no longer any restrictions in regards to the zones.

Restriction

Neither team is allowed to use long passes.

DEFENDING TACTICAL SITUATION 10

Defending Against Teams with a Three Man Defence

Defending Against Teams With A Three Man Defence

When the opposition switched to a three man defence, the two Borussia Dortmund forwards had to adjust their positioning to the new situation. They took up wider and more flat positions to be able to put pressure on all three players.

Situation 1 - Dealing with a Three Man Defence

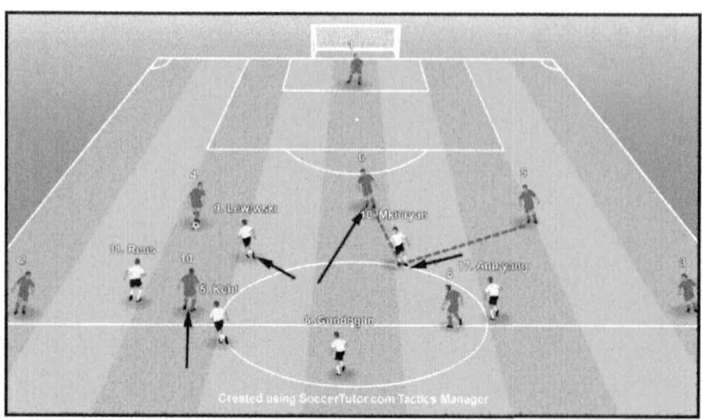

The opposition defensive midfielder (No.6) drops into a centre back's position. Mkhitaryan (10) drops a few yards back and is in line with the centre forward Lewandowski (9). This positioning enables him to control both red No.6 and No.5.

The ball is passed to red No.6 in the centre, but both Dortmund forwards stay in balanced positions in order to control the potential passes to the wide centre backs (No.4 and No.5).

The defensive midfielders Kehl (5) and Gundogan (8) try to keep the space behind the forwards limited for the opposition midfielders (No.10 and No.8) and control them at the same time.

The ball is passed to red No.5 and Mkhitaryan (10) moves close to him. Lewandowski (9) shifts across and takes a wide and flat position to control both red No.6 and No.4.

Situation 2 - Dealing with a Three Man Defence with Unbalanced Positioning (1)

The positioning of the two Borussia Dortmund forward is not balanced. Mkhitaryan (10) is too far away to close down No.5 on time. So when the ball is passed to No.5, he has available space to move forward.

No.5 moves forward with the ball and the midfielders drop back to give Mkhitaryan (10) time to close him down.

In addition, the passing lanes for the potential through balls are blocked.

Situation 3 - Dealing with a Three Man Defence with Unbalanced Positioning (2)

This is a similar situation to the previous one.

Red No.6 has the ball and Mkhitaryan (10) is away from No.5 again. However, this time the right winger Aubameyang (17) is in a more advanced position than he was in the previous situation. This positioning enables him to control both red No.5 and No.3.

As soon as the pass towards red No.5 is made, Aubameyang (17) takes advantage of the transmission phase and puts pressure on the ball in a way that prevents the pass to his direct opponent No.3. Gundogan (8) reads the tactical situation quickly and moves forward to mark red No.8 and prevent him from being the link player to direct the ball to No.3. Mkhitaryan (10) shifts towards the strong side and seeks to block a potential pass towards the inside. Lewandowski (9) also shifts towards the right.

Situation 4 - Dealing with a Pass Towards the Full Back when the Winger Was Out of Position Against a Three Man Defence

Aubameyang (17) puts pressure on red No.5 who has the ball. The red No.11 drops into a deeper position. The four Borussia Dortmund defenders keep the line compact as they retain short distances between each other.

Despite Aubameyang's pressure on the ball, No.5 passes to No.3. Piszczek (26) puts pressure on No.3 immediately due to No.11's deep position. The rest of the defenders shift towards the strong side and retain cohesion while Gundogan (8) drops back and takes over No.11's marking. The main element is that Piszczek (26) puts pressure on No.3 so that he will not be able to fully turn with the ball and analyse his available passing options. If Piszczek moves forward too late then the defending may not be successful.

In a similar situation to the previous one, red No.3 drops deeper to receive. This action lengthens the distance between Piszczek (26) and red No.3. The most suitable player to close No.3 down is the defensive midfielder Gundogan (8).

Piszczek (26) takes over red No.11's marking and Aubameyang (17) drops back to provide support to Gundogan.

DEFENDING TACTICAL SITUATION 11 

Dealing with the Extensive Shift of a Centre Back Towards the Sideline (Covering the Position)

Dealing With The Extensive Shift Of A Centre Back

When an extensive shift from one of the centre backs near the sideline took place, the team triggered certain mechanisms to deal with the situation and avoid losing balance in the defensive line.

As already mentioned, the defenders retained short distances between each other. So in cases when the full back moved into a more advanced position and the centre back had to track an opponent near the sideline, all the defenders had to shift towards the sideline.

However, this reaction would result in all of the defenders moving towards the ball area and half of the pitch would be left unoccupied and thus vulnerable to a switch of play. In order for the team to avoid this happening, the defensive midfielder who had the holding role would drop back into a centre back's position.

In this example, the build up of the red team takes place on the left side of Borussia Dortmund. The full back No.2 makes a forward run and Dortmund's left winger Reus (11) tracks him until he enters Schmelzer's (29) zone of responsibility.

In addition, Lewandowski (9) moves towards the sideline.

Red No.2 receives and passes towards the path of No.9 who continues his run towards the sideline. The Borussia Dortmund centre back Hummels (15) follows red No.11's movement and in order for the defensive line to be balanced, Kehl (the defensive midfielder) drops back into a centre back's position. This action prevents the extensive shift of all the defenders towards the strong side which would cause the line to become unbalanced.

CHAPTER 6

DEFENDING IN THE DEFENSIVE THIRD

Defending In The Defensive Third

When Borussia Dortmund had to defend within the defensive third and the ball was near the sideline, the full back together with the winger put pressure on the man in possession, while the three defenders were positioned inside the penalty area marking the players within their zone of responsibility.

The two defensive midfielders and the winger on the weak side were positioned on the edge of the penalty area to secure the central zone. The No.10 and the centre forward had advanced positions so they are ready for a potential counter attack. Borussia Dortmund had to make sure that there were always three defenders inside the penalty area, so in cases when there was an extensive shift by one of the centre backs, the gap inside the box would be filled.

Situation 1

Created using SoccerTutor.com Tactics Manager

The ball is directed to the red right winger No.7. Schmelzer (29) moves to close him down while the left winger Reus (11) drops back to help double mark him. The other three defenders take up positions inside the penalty area marking their direct opponents within their zone of responsibility, while the two defensive midfielders (together with the right winger) take up positions at the edge of the penalty area to secure the central zone. Mkhitaryan (10) is close to the opposition's defensive midfielder on the strong side and the centre forward (9) is in an advanced position.

Situation 2

Created using SoccerTutor.com Tactics Manager

In this situation, the red right winger (7) manages to receive behind the Dortmund left back Schmelzer (29).

The centre back Hummels (15) makes an extensive shift towards the sideline to contest the man in possession.

Created using SoccerTutor.com Tactics Manager

The defensive midfielder Kehl (5) enters the penalty area and takes up a centre back's position in order to fill the gap created by Hummel's (15) movement.

Double marking is applied near the sideline by the centre back Hummels (15) and the left back Schmelzer (29), while the left winger (11) shifts to just outside the box to fill the gap which was created by Kehl's movement.

The team retains balance and good shape.

CHAPTER 7

THE TRANSITION FROM ATTACK TO DEFENCE

The Transition From Attack To Defence

During the negative transition (transition from attack to defence) Borussia Dortmund applied immediate pressure on the ball most of the time, to regain possession.

In order for the team to be able to regain possession immediately, several elements were essential when carrying out the attacking phase:

1. Retaining Superiority in Numbers at the Back During the Possession Phase
2. Retaining Balance in Midfield
3. Retaining Balance Near the Sidelines to Cover for the Forward Moving Full Back
4. Retaining a Safety Player at All Times

NEGATIVE TRANSITION TACTICAL SITUATION 1

Retaining Superiority in Numbers at the Back Against the 4-4-2 Formation

Retaining Superiority In Numbers At The Back Against The 4-4-2 Formation

When playing against various formations, Borussia Dortmund's players made sure that they retained a numerical advantage at the back so they could defend aggressively and win the ball back immediately.

If there was equality or an inferiority in numbers at the back, the players did not react in an aggressive way, but instead defended in a controlled way with the aim of preventing their direct opponents from beating them in 1 v 1 duels and taking up effective defensive positions in case possession was lost.

Retaining numerical superiority at the back was obtained through various ways and depended on the number of opposition forwards.

Situation 1 - The Full Back Drops into a Deeper Position

The defensive midfielder Sahin (18 has the ball in midfield. As there are two opposition forwards in advanced positions, the weak side's full back Schmelzer (29) drops back to be in line with the deeper red forward (No.10) and creates a 3 v 2 situation at the back. Additionally, this position enables him to drop further back and take up an effective defensive position in case possession is lost.

Situation 2 - The Defensive Midfielder Drops into a Deeper Position Between the Two Opposition Forwards

In this situation both of Borussia Dortmund's full backs are in advanced positions.

The defensive midfielder Kehl (5) reads the tactical situation and drops back to be in line with red No.10 to create a 3 v 2 situation.

Situation 3 - The Defensive Midfielder Drops into a Centre Back's Position to Help Move the Ball Forward

In this situation the defensive midfielder Sahin (18) has dropped back to create a three man defence in order to help the centre backs to move the ball forward more easily. This creates a 3 v 2 situation and as well as helping move the ball forward, the team has a spare player at the back and is ready to defend aggressively in case possession is lost.

Kehl (5) moves into a balanced position in the centre. Another option for the defensive midfielder was to drop deeper in between the two centre backs.

Session For This Tactical Situation *(5 Practices)*

1. Retaining Superiority in Numbers at the Back Against the 4-4-2 in a Simple 2 Zone 4 v 2 Practice

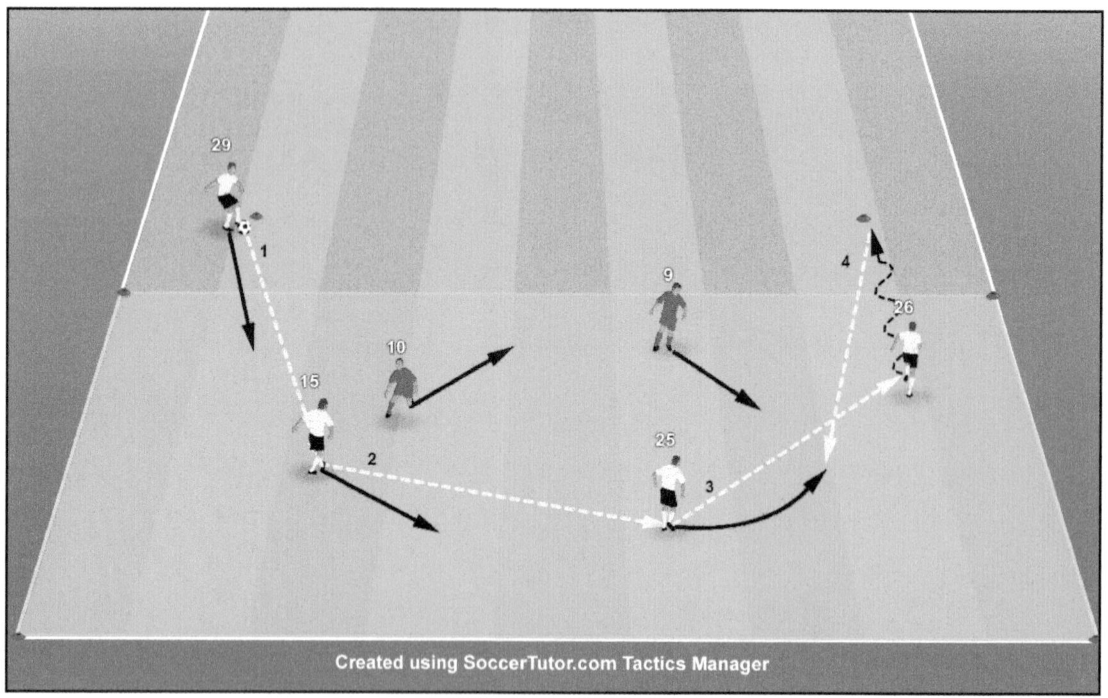

Objective

The defenders work on maintaining a numerical advantage at the back against two forwards.

Description

In a 30 x 20 yards, three yellow defenders and two red forwards start inside the low zone. The practice starts with the yellow full back (No.29) who is positioned on the blue cone. The red forwards defend in a passive way as the yellow defenders pass the ball to the other side's full back (No.26) who receives and moves forward.

As soon as No.26 moves out of the first zone, the weak side's full back (No.29) moves into line with the deeper positioned red forward in order to create a 3 v 2 situation. Additionally, the other defenders move according to the new position of the ball. As soon as No.26 reaches the blue cone, he passes back and the ball is then directed towards the other side with the same aim in the opposite direction. There should always be a 3 v 2 situation inside the first zone.

Coaching Points

1. The players need to make sure all their passes are accurate to replicate real match situations.
2. There needs to be good synchronisation in the players' movements, so as soon as one full back moves forward, the other one needs to drop back to maintain the 3 v 2 advantage.

PROGRESSION

2. Retaining Superiority in Numbers when Both Full Backs are in Advanced Positions (Def. Midfielder Drops Back)

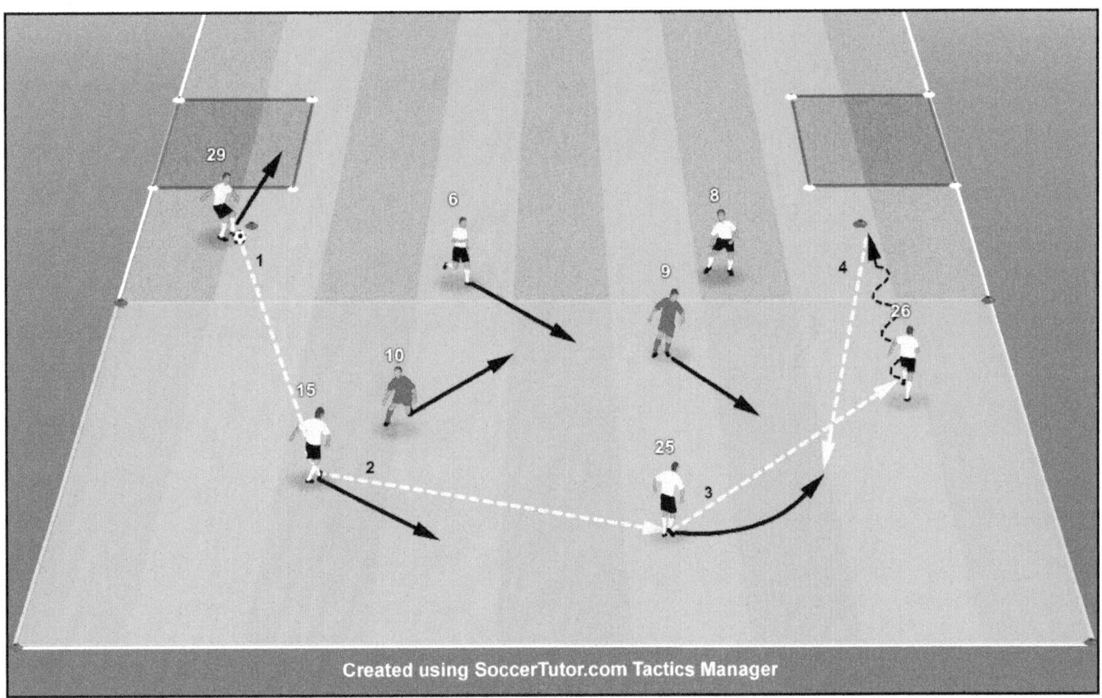

Description

This is a progression of the previous practice and we add two yellow defensive midfielders who take up positions in the high zone. With the addition of the defensive midfielders, it enables both full backs to be in advanced positions at the same time.

After the full back passes the ball to the centre back, he now has the option of moving inside the dark blue zone (advanced position).

The weak side's defensive midfielder (No.6 in diagram) must be aware of the full back's positioning in order to drop back (in line with the deeper positioned red forward) to maintain the 3 v 2 numerical advantage at the back. If the full back decides to enter the low zone as in the previous practice, there is no need for the defensive midfielder to drop back.

There should always be a 3 v 2 situation inside the low zone, whether it is the weak side's full back or a defensive midfielder who drops back.

PROGRESSION

3. Retaining Superiority In Numbers at the Back Against the 4-4-2 in a 6 v 4 Dynamic 4 Zone Transition Game

Created using SoccerTutor.com Tactics Manager

Description

This is a progression of the previous practice. After the full back receives and moves forward out of the low zone, instead of passing back, he makes a pass to the strong side's defensive midfielder (No.8 in diagram). The defensive midfielder then passes towards one of the mini goals.

The respective red player (the same side as the goal) positioned on the yellow cone dribbles forward and passes towards one of the red forwards in the low zone. The aim for the reds is to dribble the ball through the red end line. The yellow defenders must react and try to win the ball. If the full back on the weak side is inside the dark blue zone, the midfielder should drop back to create a 3 v 2 situation.

Restrictions

1. Only the yellow players inside the low zone can take part when defending. Only the two red forwards are allowed inside the low zone.
2. The midfielders inside the white middle zone do not contest the red player who moves forward.
3. There can be a restriction of 6 seconds for the yellows to win the ball back.

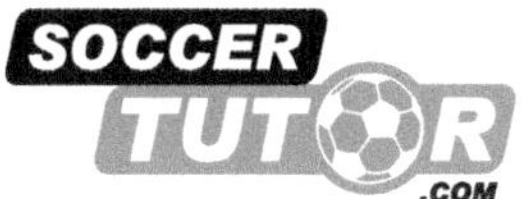

PROGRESSION

4. Retaining Superiority in Numbers at the Back Against the 4-4-2 in a 6 v 4 Dynamic 4 Zone Transition Game (2)

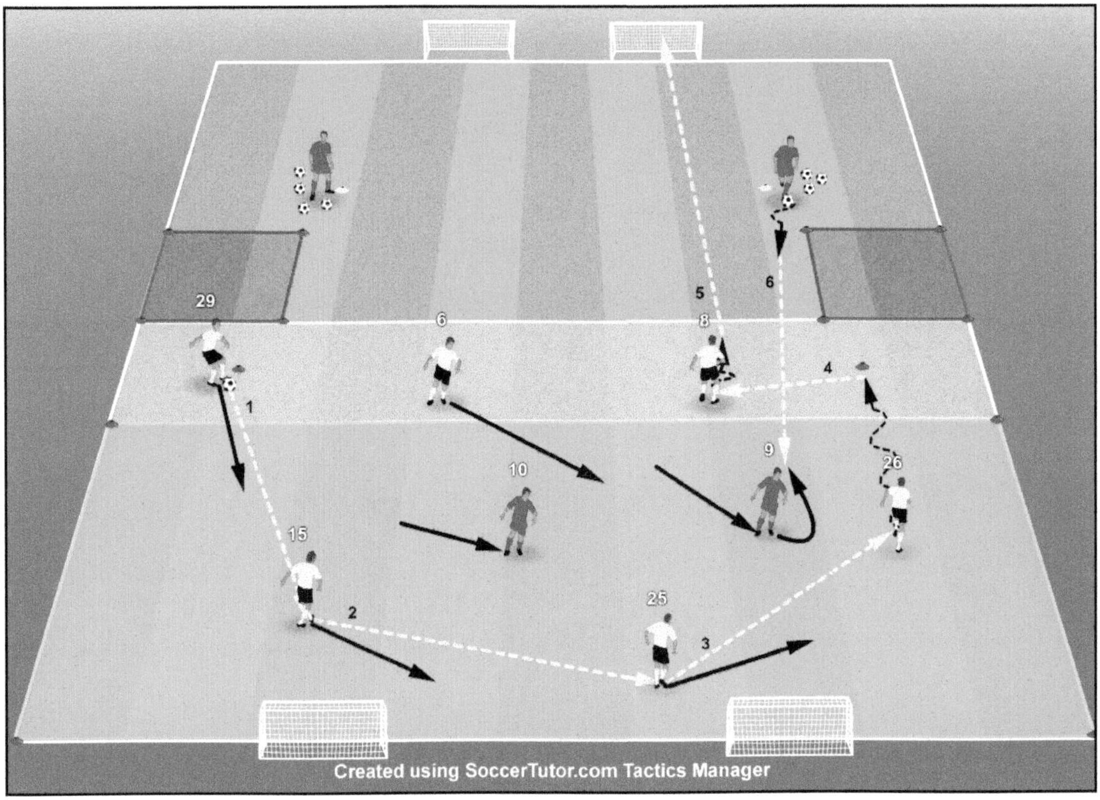
29
6
8
5
6
4
1
9
10
26
15
25
2
3
Created using SoccerTutor.com Tactics Manager

Description

This is a progression of the previous practice with the same restrictions.

The only difference this time is that the red forwards have the aim of scoring in one of the two mini goals which makes it harder for the yellow players to defend.

PROGRESSION

5. Retaining Superiority in Numbers at the Back and Transition Play in an 8 v 8 Small Sided Game

Created using SoccerTutor.com Tactics Manager

Description

We play an 8 v 8 small sided game in a 40 x 50 yard area. There are two red forwards and four yellow defenders in the low zone (40 x 20 yards).

The aim of the yellow team is to score, but they should always retain superiority in numbers inside the low zone in order to defend successfully in case possession is lost. The red players try to win possession in the high zone and then direct the ball immediately towards one of the two forwards inside the blue low zone with the aim of scoring a goal.

Restrictions

1. The two red forwards play passively when defending against the yellow defenders in the low zone.
2. The yellow midfielders do not try to prevent passes towards the red forwards after losing possession.
3. Only the two red forwards are allowed inside the low zone.
4. There can be a restriction of 6 seconds for the yellows to win the ball back.

NEGATIVE TRANSITION TACTICAL SITUATION 2

Retaining Superiority in Numbers at the Back Against the 4-2-3-1 Formation

Retaining Superiority In Numbers At The Back Against The 4-2-3-1 Formation

When playing against one opposition forward and one attacking midfielder (No.10), Borussia Dortmund's players had to adjust their positioning according to the attacking midfielder's positioning. If the player was in an advanced position, Dortmund had to react as against the 4-4-2 formation.

This was not the case if the opposition No.10's positioning was deeper and in between the two Boussia Dortmund defensive midfielders. Their reaction was different then.

Situation 1 - The Full Back Drops into a Deeper Position

As the red No.10 is in an advanced position, there is a 2 v 2 situation at the back. To compensate for this, Borussia Dortmund's full back on the weak side Schmelzer (29) drops back in line with the deeper positioned red forward (No.10).

Situation 2 - The Defensive Midfielder Drops into a Deeper Position Between the Two Opposition Forwards

In this situation the red team's No.10 has an advanced position behind Borussia Dortmund's defensive midfielders again.

As both full backs (No.26 and No.29) are in advanced positions, the defensive midfielder No.6 reads the tactical situation and drops back to create a 3 v 2 numerical advantage at the back.

Situation 3 - The Opposition Attacking Midfielder is in a Deep Position Between the Two Borussia Dortmund Defensive Midfielders

In this situation the positioning of the opposition No.10 is in between the two Borussia Dortmund defensive midfielders.

As a result of this, a 2 v 1 situation is created at the back. No additional action is required for Borussia Dortmund.

Situation 4 - The Defensive Midfielder Drops into a Deeper Position Between the Two Opposition Forwards

As the centre back Sokratis (25) is under the red No.9's pressure, the defensive midfielder Sahin (18) drops back to provide a passing option.

Despite No.10's advanced positioning, a numerical advantage (3 v 2) is created for Borussia Dortmund at the back.

Session For This Tactical Situation *(2 Practices)*

1. Retaining Superiority in Numbers at the Back Against the 4-2-3-1 in a Simple 2 Zone 4 v 2 Practice

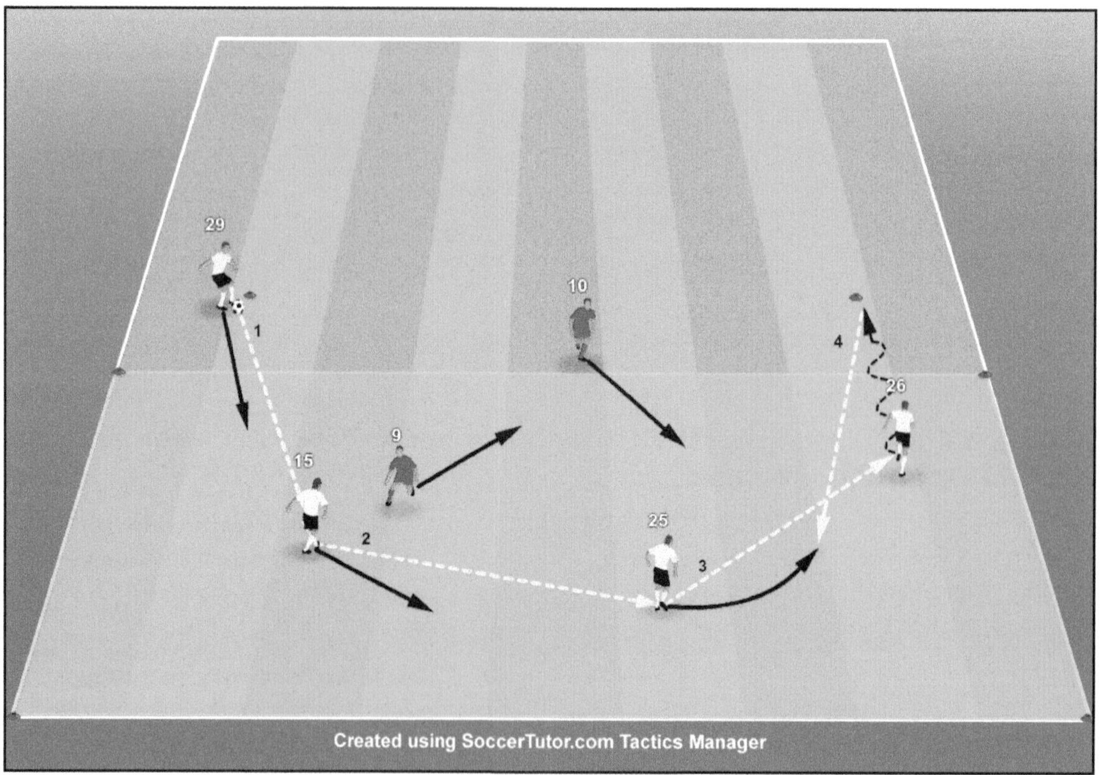

Objective

The defenders work on maintaining a numerical advantage at the back against one forward and a No.10.

Description

If the opposition use the 4-2-3-1 formation, the previous practices from 'Retaining Superiority in Numbers at the Back Against the 4-4-2 Formation' can be adjusted to this formation.

The defenders pass the ball to each other until it reaches the full back who moves forward up to the blue cone and passes back. The red No.10 who is positioned in the high zone decides whether or not to enter the low zone. If he enters, then the weak side's full back (No.29 in diagram) must drop back to create a numerical advantage. If the No.10 does not drop, there is no need for No.29 to drop back as a 2 v 1 situation already exists. There should always be a numerical superiority inside the low zone.

Coaching Points

1. The players need to make sure all their passes are accurate to replicate real match situations.
2. The full back on the weak side needs to be able to read the tactical situation and act quickly.

PROGRESSION

2. Retaining Superiority in Numbers when Both Full Backs are in Advanced Positions (Def. Midfielder Drops Back)

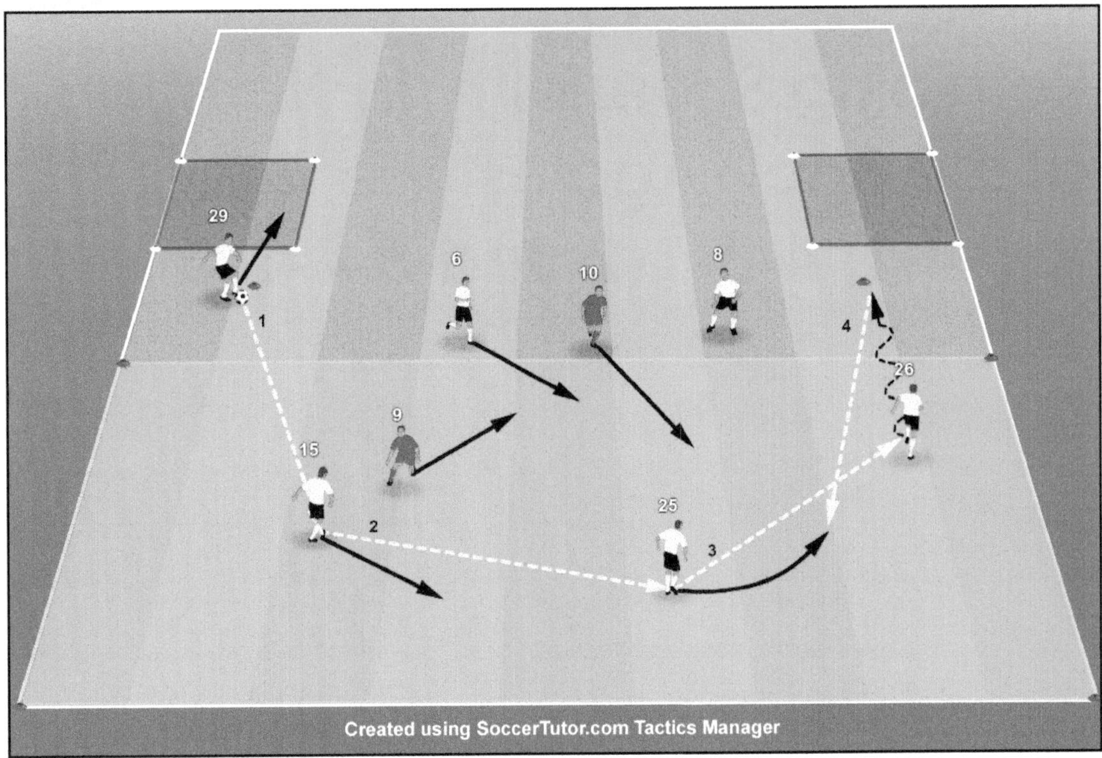

Description

In this progression, two yellow midfielders are added.

This time the full back has the option of staying in an advanced position inside the dark blue zone, so the weak side's defensive midfielder has to drop back.

If the full back drops back, there is no need for the defensive midfielder to drop back into the low zone. There should always be a numerical advantage inside the low zone (3 v 2 or 2 v 1).

NEGATIVE TRANSITION TACTICAL SITUATION 3

Retaining Superiority in Numbers at the Back Against the 4-3-3, 4-1-4-1, 4-3-1-2 and 3-4-1-2

Retaining Superiority In Numbers At The Back Against The 4-3-3 Or 4-1-4-1 Formation

When playing against one opposition forward things were more simple as the two Borussia Dortmund centre backs already provided a numerical advantage (2 v 1).

Situation 1a - Two Centre Backs Against One Opposition Forward

The defensive midfielder Sahin (18) has the ball in midfield and the two Borussia Dortmund centre backs have to deal with one forward.

In this 2 v 1 situation no additional action is required.

Situation 1b - Against One Opposition Forward: The Defensive Midfielder Drops Back to Cover for the Centre Back Moving into an Advanced Position

The centre back Sokratis (25) moves forward with the ball and as the situation at the back turns to 1 v 1, the defensive midfielder Sahin (18) drops deeper into a centre back's position and creates a 2 v 1.

Retaining Superiority In Numbers At The Back Against The 4-3-1-2 Or 3-4-1-2 Formation

When playing against teams that used two forwards and one attacking midfielder i.e. 4-3-1-2 & 3-4-1-2, there were times when Dortmund's defenders had to deal with three players in advanced positions.

Situation 1a - Dealing with Two Forwards and a Deeper Positioned Attacking Midfielder Against the 4-3-1-2 Formation

The defensive midfielder Sahin (18) has the ball in midfield while the opposition attacking midfielder (No.10) has a position between the two Borussia Dortmund defensive midfielders.

So the centre backs now have to deal with two forwards in a 2 v 2 situation. That is why the weak side's full back Schmelzer (29) drops back in line with No.11 and helps create a 3 v 2 situation at the back.

Situation 1b - Dealing with Two Forwards and a Deeper Positioned Attacking Midfielder Against the 3-4-1-2 Formation

In a similar situation against the 3-4-1-2 formation (with the red wing backs No.3 and No.7 in wide positions), the Borussia Dortmund left back Schmelzer (29) drops again back to create a 3 v 2 situation at the back.

Situation 2a - The Defensive Midfielder Creates Superiority in Numbers by Dropping Deeper Against the 4-3-1-2

In this situation both Borussia Dortmund full backs are in advanced positions. The defensive midfielder Bender (6) reads the tactical situation and drops back to create a 3 v 2 situation at the back.

Situation 2b - The Defensive Midfielder Creates Superiority in Numbers by Dropping Deeper Against the 3-4-1-2 Formation

This is the same situation as the previous one against the 3-4-1-2 formation.

Situation 3a - The Defensive Midfielder Drops into a Centre Back's Position to Help the Defenders Move the Ball Forward Against the 4-3-1-2 Formation

In this situation the defensive midfielder Sahin (18) drops back to help the defenders to move the ball forward.

This creates a numerical superiority at the back (3 v 2).

Situation 3b - The Defensive Midfielder Drops into a Centre Back's Position to Help the Defenders Move the Ball Forward Against the 3-4-1-2 Formation

This is a similar situation to the previous one against the 3-4-1-2 formation.

Situation 4a - Both the Full Back and the Defensive Midfielder Drop Deeper to Create Superiority in Numbers Against the 4-3-1-2 Formation

In this situation the opposition's attacking midfielder is in an advanced position.

This creates a 2 v 3 or 3 v 3 situation at the back and forces both the weak side's full back and the defensive midfielder (6) to drop back to create a numerical advantage.

Situation 4b - Both the Full Back and the Defensive Midfielder Drop Deeper to Create Superiority in Numbers Against the 3-4-1-2 Formation

This is the same situation as the previous one against the 3-4-1-2 formation.

Situation 5a - Defensive Midfielder Drops into Centre Back's Position and the Full Back on the Weak Side Creates Superiority in Numbers Against the 4-3-1-2 Formation

The defensive midfielder Sahin (18) drops into a centre back's position and as the opposition attacking midfielder has an advanced position and there is still equality in numbers, the weak side's full back (29) drops deeper to help create a 4 v 3 situation at the back.

Situation 5b - Defensive Midfielder Drops into Centre Back's Position and the Full Back on the Weak Side Creates Superiority in Numbers Against the 3-4-1-2 Formation

This is the same situation as the previous one against the 3-4-1-2 formation.

Situation 6a - Defensive Midfielder Drops into Centre Back's Position and the Other Defensive Midfielder Creates Superiority in Numbers Against the 4-3-1-2 Formation

In this situation the second defensive midfielder (6) drops back to help create a numerical advantage.

Situation 6b - Defensive Midfielder Drops into Centre Back's Position and the Other Defensive Midfielder Creates Superiority in Numbers Against the 3-4-1-2 Formation

This is the same situation as the previous one against the 3-4-1-2 formation.

NEGATIVE TRANSITION TACTICAL SITUATION 4

Retaining Balance in Midfield

Retaining Balance In Midfield

Retaining balance in the midfield line enabled Borussia Dortmund to apply immediate pressure on the ball after losing possession. However, the retaining of balance in midfield depended on how superiority in numbers was obtained at the back. In the diagrams to follow we provide an analysis of how balance in the midfield was retained during the possession phase.

Superiority In Numbers At The Back Created By The Full Back Dropping Back On The Weak Side

Borussia Dortmund have created a three man defence with the weak side's full back (29) dropping back. The centre back Sokratis(25) has the ball and is ready to pass forward, while the opposition midfielders take up defensive positions to intercept the potential pass.

The three red midfielders No.6, No.8 and No.11 (more likely No.8 and No.11) are the players who have the best chances of intercepting the forward pass. The positioning of the two Borussia Dortmund defensive midfielders and the full back enables them to control and apply immediate pressure on all three red midfielders (No.6, No.8 and No.11) inside the blue marked area if they win possession.

It must be mentioned that the right back Piszczek (26) makes sure not to take up a risky position against his direct opponent No.11, which enables him to put pressure on No.11 if possession is lost or even move forward if there is a Dortmund midfielder free of marking ready to pass forward. However, this positioning does not help Dortmund to create a numerical advantage on the flank.

Tactical Analysis: 3 Man Defence Created By The Full Back On The Weak Side Dropping Back

Situation 1

The centre back Sokratis (25) makes the forward pass, but the opposition's midfielder No.6 intercepts the ball.

Sahin (18) applies pressure on No.6 forcing him towards the sideline and Bender (6) drops to cover. The right back Piszczek (26) converges towards the centre and marks his direct opponent No.11 who is a potential receiver. As red No.9 moves towards a potential passing lane, Sokratis (25) moves to mark him closely so he can pressure aggressively if the pass is directed to him. Hummels (15) drops to cover No.25's position and Schmelzer (29) moves towards the centre to keep the 3 man defence compact and retain superiority in numbers.

Situation 2

This time the red winger (11) is the player who intercepts the forward pass from Sokratis (25).

As the right back Piszczek (26) has an effective position, he moves to put pressure on the man in possession immediately.

Sokratis (25) marks red No.9 from a close distance as he is a potential receiver and Sahin (18) moves close to the ball area to provide support.

The 3 v 2 is retained at the back and the defenders can mark their direct opponents aggressively.

Tactical Analysis: Superiority In Numbers Created By Def. Midfielder Dropping Back

In this situation, as the full back Schmelzer (29) on the weak side is in an advanced position, the defensive midfielder Bender (6) is the player who creates superiority in numbers at the back by dropping deeper.

Bender is focused on controlling red No.10 rather than putting immediate pressure on red No.6. This forces Sahin (18) to control both red No.6 and No.8. The right back Piszczek (26) controls No.11.

Situation 1

The pass from Sokratis (25) is intercepted by the red midfielder No.8.

Sahin (18) puts immediate pressure on the new man in possession (red No.6) and forces him towards the side. The right back Piszczek (26) converges and marks his direct opponent No.11 and Sokratis (25) marks No.9 at a close distance. Bender (6) is close to No.10 who moves to provide a passing option towards the inside. Hummels (15) moves into a covering position for both Sokratis and Bender. Superiority in numbers is ensured at the back so the left back Schmelzer (29) does not have to drop further back, but instead shifts into a controlling position.

Situation 2

The forward pass is intercepted by red No.11 this time.

Both Sahin and the right back Piszczek (26) apply immediate pressure on the new man in possession.

Sokratis (25) marks red No.9 closely as he is a potential receiver and Hummels (15) shifts into a covering position.

Bender (6) drops back to ensure there is superiority in numbers in defence.

Tactical Analysis: Superiority In Numbers Created By The Def. Midfielder Dropping Back Into A Centre Back's Position

In this situation, the defensive midfielder Sahin (18) drops into a centre back's position.

The other defensive midfielder Bender (6) moves into a central position and controls both red No.6 and No.8. The right back Piszczek (26) controls No.11.

Situation 2

The forward pass from Sahin (18) is intercepted by red No.8.

The defensive midfielder Bender (6) moves to put pressure on the ball and the right back Piszczek (26) marks red No.11. The other defensive midfielder Sahin (18) moves to mark red No.9 closely.

Sokratis (25) moves into a covering position for Sahin and Hummels (15) shifts to provide compactness in the back three. He also ensures that there is a numerical superiority at the back.

Session For This Tactical Situation *(3 Practices)*

1. Retaining Balance in the Midfield Line to Prepare for the Transition From Attack to Defence 6 v 6 Zonal Game

Created using SoccerTutor.com Tactics Manager

Objective

Retaining balance in midfield and preparing for the negative transition with intelligent positioning.

Description

The yellow defenders retain possession and aim to retain a numerical advantage when the strong side full back moves forward (either the weak side full back or defensive midfielder drop back) inside the low zone, overcome the opposition forwards' pressure and then score in the three mini goals.

The 4 red midfielders inside the white zone try to intercept the passes towards the mini goals and move forward with the ball with the aim of either dribbling through the central red line (2 points) or pass the ball to one of the forwards inside the low zone who then try to dribble the ball through the red end line (1 point). If the reds achieve both of these aims they get 2 bonus points.

Restrictions

1. Only the red midfielder who intercepts the ball can move out of the white zone.
2. Only one yellow full back or defensive midfielder is allowed in the low zone when the yellows are in possession (3 v 2 situation). The others must remain in their zone.

PROGRESSION

2. Retaining Balance in the Midfield Line to Prepare for the Transition From Attack to Defence 6 v 6 Zonal Game (2)

Created using SoccerTutor.com Tactics Manager

Description

This is a progression of the previous practice.

The teams have the same aims and restrictions, but the difference is that the red forwards now try to score in the two mini goals we have added (instead of dribbling through the end red line).

Coaching Points

1. The yellow players need to have quick and cohesive reactions to losing possession.
2. Players need to be able to read the specific tactical situation and good accurate passing should be maintained throughout the practice.
3. The synchronisation in the players' movements is important, especially when the strong side's full back moves forward, a player needs to drop back immediately to retain the 3 v 2 advantage at the back.

PROGRESSION

3.Retaining Balance in the Midfield Line to Prepare for the Transition From Attack to Defence 6 v 6 Zonal Game (3)

Description

This is another progression. The same aims and restrictions apply again, but now the red forwards try to score against the goalkeeper in a full sized goal.

ASSESSMENT:

The practices for this tactical situation can be adjusted to different formations.

NEGATIVE TRANSITION TACTICAL SITUATION 5

Retaining Balance Near the Sideline

Retaining Balance Near The Sideline

As has been already mentioned, Borussia Dortmund usually attacked with four forwards (centre forward and three attacking midfielders) plus one full back who moved into an advanced position. The team had to retain balance near the sideline where the full back made a forward run in order to be ready for a successful negative transition.

The Full Back And Winger Are In Advanced Positions And The Def. Midfielder Provides Balance

In this tactical situation, Borussia Dortmund's three man defence is created by the weak side full back's deep position (the left back - No.29). The centre back Sokratis (25) has the ball and moves forward.

The winger Aubameyang (17) drops back to create space, and at the same time Piszczek (26) makes a forward run (synchronised with Aubameyang's movement). As Piszczek is already in an advanced position and Aubameyang is in between the lines, the defensive midfielder Sahin (18) has to control both red No.8 and No.11 in order for the team to be able to carry out a successful negative transition on the flank.

Tactical Analysis: The Balance Near The Sideline Is Provided By The Def. Midfielder

Situation 1

Red No.8 intercepts the forward pass.

The defensive midfielder Sahin (18) puts pressure on the ball and Aubameyang (17) drops back to help double mark him. Piszczek (26) drops back immediately to control his direct opponent who moves forward. The centre back Sokratis (25) has to control the pass towards No.9 and the forward pass to No.11 until Piszczek drops into an effective defensive position.

No.15 provides cover for No.25 and No.29 (3 man defence / superiority in numbers).

Red No.8 passes to No.11, before Piszczek (26) manages to drop back into an effective defensive position.

Sokratis (25) has to play for time to allow Piszczek to recover.

Hummels (15) and Schmelzer (29) form a compact three man defence and Bender (6) drops back to be close to them.

This time red No.8 makes a forward pass towards No.11. Sokratis (25) has to evaluate the situation and decide if he can intervene successfully. Sokratis decides to intervene in order to intercept the pass. Hummels (15) and Schmelzer (29) move towards the strong side (chain reaction) and Bender (6) drops further back and close to the defenders to compensate for the extensive shift of Sokratis towards the sideline. This position enables him to drop between the defenders (according to the tactical situation).

Situation 2

Red No.11 intercepts the forward pass.

Sahin (18) moves to apply immediate pressure on red No.11 and Piszczek (26) drops back.

Sokratis (25) marks red No.9 who is a potential receiver. Aubameyang (17) drops into a defensive midfielder's position to retain balance.

Tactical Analysis: Full Back Moves Forward & The Winger Drops Deep To Provide Balance

Situation 1

In this tactical situation the left winger Aubameyang (17) has dropped back into a deeper position. This positioning enables him to control red No.11 and No.8.

The defensive midfielder Sahin (18) can move into an advanced position and Borussia Dortmund have five players in advanced positions ready to take part in the attack.

Red No.11 intercepts the forward pass.

Aubameyang (17) puts pressure on the man in possession (red No.11) and Piszczek (26) drops back to help double mark him.

Sokratis (25) marks red No.9 closely. Hummels (15) provides cover for Sokratis and the left back Schmelzer (29) ensures compactness and superiority in numbers at the back.

Situation 2

In this tactical situation, Borussia Dortmund's three man defence is created by the defensive midfielder Sahin (18) dropping back into a centre back's position. The other defensive midfielder Bender (6) moves into a central position. Sahin (18) has the ball on the right. As Bender is too far away to control red No.11, the right winger Aubameyang (17) should drop into a deeper position which enables him to control No.11 in case he intercepts the potential forward pass. Additionally, Aubameyang controls the red midfielder No.8.

Red No.8 intercepts the forward pass.

Aubameyang (17) applies immediate pressure on the man in possession (red No.8). Piszczek (26) drops back and Sokratis (25) marks red No.9 who moves towards a potential passing lane. Sahin (18) and Hummels (15) provide cover.

Sahin (18) should keep an eye on the forward moving red No.11 until Piszczek manages to drop into an effective defensive position.

Situation 3

Red No.11 intercepts the forward pass.

Aubameyang (17) applies immediate pressure on red No.11 and the right back Piszczek (26) drops back.

Sahin (18) marks red No.9 and Sokratis (25)shifts across to cover his position and Hummels (15) shifts across to ensure compactness and a numerical superiority at the back.

Tactical Analysis: The Full Back & Winger Are In Advanced Positions And The Def. Midfielder Drops Back To Provide Balance

In this tactical situation both the right back Piszczek (26) and the right winger Aubameyang (17) are in advanced positions. This positioning of Aubameyang enables him to control red No.8, but not No.11 (the closest player to him is Sahin). In order for Borussia Dortmund to retain superiority in numbers at the back, the defensive midfielder Bender (6) drops. If red No.11 intercepts the forward pass, Sahin (18) can then move forward to put pressure on him as Bender (6) can drop further and ensure there is a spare player at the back.

Red No.11 intercepts the forward pass.

Sahin (18) moves to close red No.11 down and play for time so his teammates are able to recover and create a numerical advantage at the back.

Additionally, time is given to both Aubameyang (17) and Piszczek (26) to drop back and contest the man in possession. Only if red No.11 makes a bad first touch can Sahin contest him (as this will make intercepting the ball highly probable).

Session For This Tactical Situation *(3 Practices)*

1. Retaining Balance Near the Sideline to Prepare for the Negative Transition in a Dynamic 8 Zone Transition Game

Objective

Retaining balance near the sideline and preparing for the negative transition with intelligent positioning.

Description

In this practice the yellow defenders aim to retain a numerical superiority inside the low zone (40 x 20 yards), overcome the opposition's forwards' pressure and score in the mini goals near the sidelines.

When there is available time and space for the defender in possession and he is able to pass towards the goal, the strong side's full back moves forward into the yellow zone and the winger drops back. The yellow players try to deal with the advanced position of the full back and retain balance near the sideline in order to carry out a successful negative transition (according to the tactical situation).

The red player inside the red zone tries to intercept the pass towards the mini goal and then move forward with the ball, aiming to either dribble the ball through the red line near the sideline (2 points) or pass the ball to one of the forwards inside the low zone who then try to dribble the ball through the red end line (1 point). If the reds achieve both of these aims they get 2 bonus points.

Once the full back on the strong side (No.29 in diagram) moves into an advanced position, the superiority at the back can be achieved by either the weak side's full back dropping back or the defensive midfielder dropping into a centre back's position.

The white arrows show the reaction of the players after the red team win possession.

Restrictions

1. The red midfielder is only allowed to move out of the red zone after intercepting the ball.
2. Only one yellow full back or defensive midfielder is allowed in the low zone at once when the yellows are in possession (3 v 2 situation).
3. When the forward pass is made, the full back on the strong side (No.29 in diagram) should be inside the yellow zone.

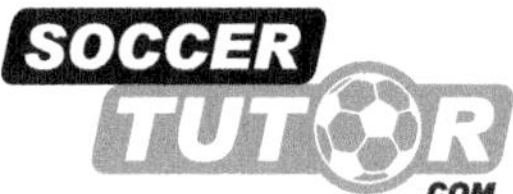

PROGRESSION

2. Retaining Balance Near the Sideline to Prepare for the Negative Transition in a Dynamic 8 Zone Transition Game (2)

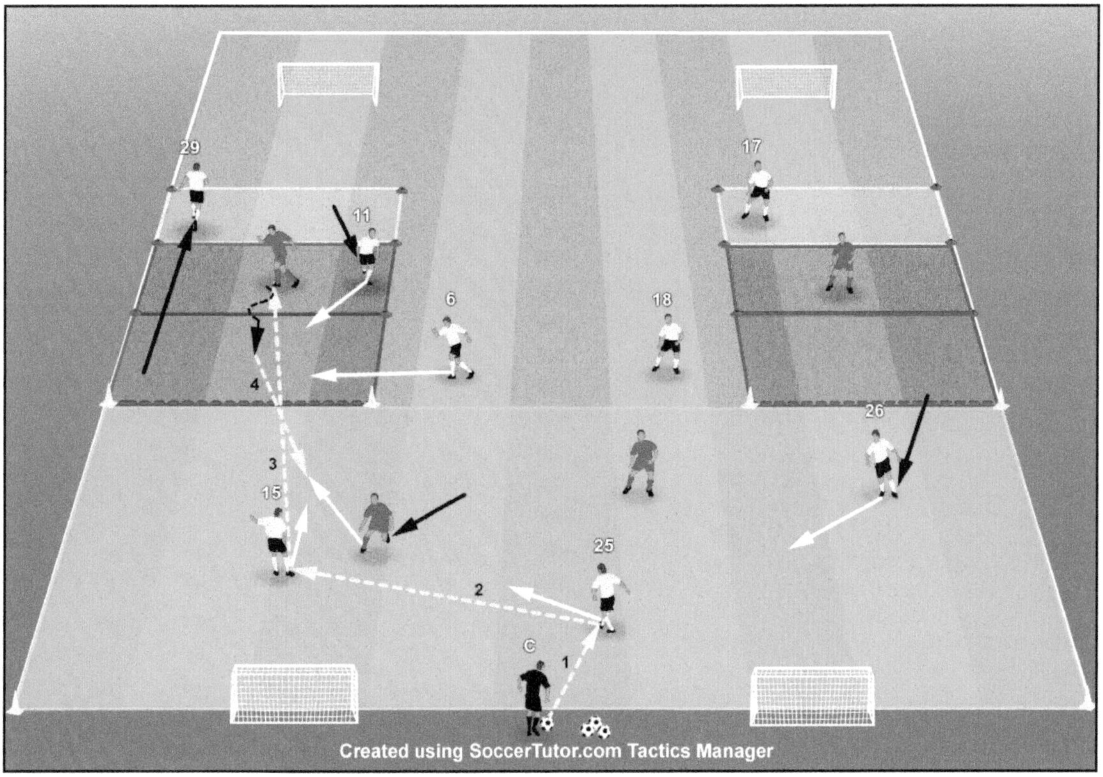
29
11
17
6
18
4
26
3
15
25
2
C
1
Created using SoccerTutor.com Tactics Manager

Description

This is a progression of the previous practice with the same aims and restrictions.

The only difference is that the red forwards try to score in two mini goals after receiving from their teammates.

Coaching Points

1. The yellow players need to have quick and cohesive reactions to losing possession.
2. Players need to be able to read the specific tactical situation and produce good accurate passing throughout the practice.
3. The synchronisation in the players' movements is important, especially when the strong side's full back moves forward, a player needs to drop back immediately to retain the 3 v 2 advantage at the back.

PROGRESSION

3. Retaining Balance Near the Sideline to Prepare for the Negative Transition in a Dynamic 8 Zone Transition Game (3)

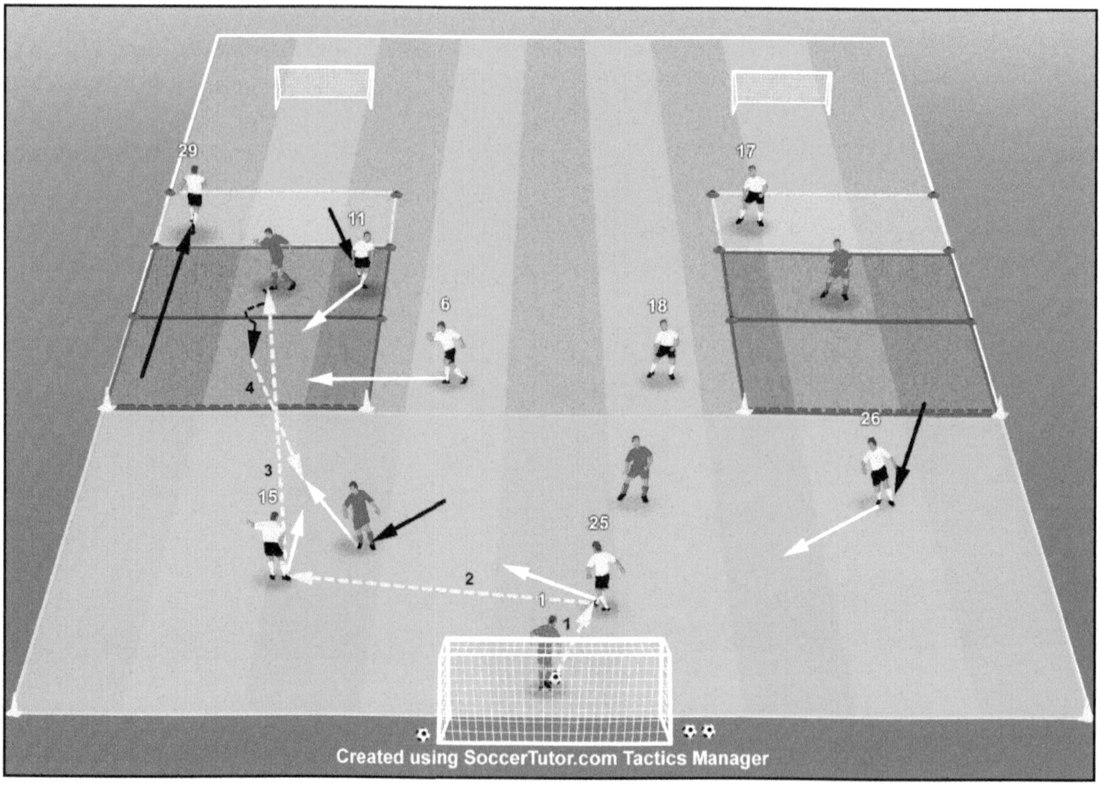

Created using SoccerTutor.com Tactics Manager

Description

This is another progression with the same aims and restrictions.

The difference is that the red forwards try to score against the goalkeeper in the full sized goal after receiving from their teammates.

ASSESSMENT:

The practices for this tactical situation can be adjusted to different formations.

NEGATIVE TRANSITION TACTICAL SITUATION 6

Retaining a Safety Player

Retaining A Safety Player

When Borussia Dortmund's players managed to move the ball to the forwards, they had at least one safety player so they were able to apply immediate pressure on the ball if possession was lost. The safety player was usually positioned deeper and in a diagonal position (according to the man in possession).

he positioning of the safety player meant he was able to provide a passing option in case a forward pass was not possible and also to apply immediate pressure on the ball if the player who had the ball lost possession.

The distance of the safety player from the man in possession has to be short enough to apply pressure on the ball. If the distance from the man in possession was larger than it should have been, Borussia Dortmund's players tried to force the ball towards the sidelines after losing possession, to delay the opposition so they could then take up effective defensive positions.

Tactical Analysis: The Full Back And Def. Midfielder Are The Safety Players

Option 1

In this situation Borussia Dortmund form a three man defence with the weak side's full back (No.29) dropping back.

The ball is in the right winger Blaszczykowski's (16) possession and both the right back Piszczek (26) and the defensive midfielder Sahin (18) are safety players.

Tactical Situation 1

The centre back Sokratis (25) makes the forward pass. Aubameyang (17) receives and moves towards the inside with the ball.

During Aubameyang's attacking movement, Sahin (18) and Piszczek (26) are the safety players.

The red No.3 tackles Aubameyang (17) and passes the ball to No.8. Sahin (who is the closest player) to the new man in possession immediately puts pressure on the ball.

Mkhitaryan (10) moves to help double mark No.8. Piszczek (26) marks No.11 and Sokratis (25) marks No.10 who are potential receivers of the ball.

Option 2

In this situation Borussia Dortmund form a three man defence with the defensive midfielder Sahin (18) dropping into a centre back's position.

The ball is in the right winger Blaszczykowski's (16) possession and both the right back Piszczek (26) and the defensive midfielder Bender (6) are safety players.

Tactical Situation 2

The ball is passed to the right winger Blaszczykowski (16) who drops back and turns towards the inside.

The right back Piszczek (26) and the defensive midfielder Bender (6) (who moves towards the strong side) are the safety players.

Red No.3 wins the ball and passes it to No.8. Bender (6) puts immediate pressure on the ball and Piszczek (26) marks red No.11.

Additionally, Sahin (18) marks red No.9 closely who is a potential receiver.

The defensive line is compact and there is superiority in numbers at the back (3 v 2).

Tactical Analysis: The Winger Receives Near The Sideline & The Full Back Is The Safety Player

Option

The ball is in the right winger Blaszczykowski's (16) possession who is positioned near the sideline this time.

The right back Piszczek (26) is the safety player and that is why the defensive midfielder Sahin (18) is able to take up a more advanced position.

Tactical Situation

The centre back Sokratis (25) directs the ball to the right winger Blaszczykowski (16) who is positioned near the sideline. Blaszczykowski receives and moves towards the inside.

The full back (Piszczek) moves towards the inside into a safety player's position and the defensive midfielder Sahin (18) moves a few yards forward.

The other defensive midfielder Bender (6) moves into a balanced position.

As soon as red No.3 tackles Blaszczykowski and passes the ball to No.11, the full back Piszczek (26) moves to close him down and Sahin (18) does the same to help double mark him.

Sokratis (25) marks red No.9 closely and Bender (6) shifts into a position to cover Piszczek's position.

Tactical Analysis: The Def. Midfielder Is The Safety Player

Option 1

The full back overlaps, but the defensive midfielder Sahin (18) is still in a safety player's position.

Tactical Situation 1

The centre back Sokratis (25) makes the forward pass. The right winger Aubameyang (17) receives and moves towards the inside. The full back Piszczek (26) makes the overlapping run.

The red No.3 tackles Aubameyang (17) and passes the ball to No.11. Sahin immediately puts pressure on the ball while Piszczek (26) recovers quickly and tries to help double mark No.11. Mkhitaryan (10) shifts across to mark red No.6 and Sokratis (25) marks red No.10.

Both red No.6 and No.10 are potential receivers of the ball. Hummels (15) provides cover for Sokratis (25) and Schmelzer (29) keeps the line compact and ensures superiority in numbers at the back.

Option 2

This is a progression of the previous situation. The full back makes an under lapping run and the defensive midfielder Sahin (18) drops back diagonally to be the safety player.

Tactical Situation

The centre back Sokratis (25) directs the ball to the right winger Blaszczykowski (16) who is positioned near the sideline.

The full back Piszczek (26) makes the under lapping run to take advantage of the space in behind red No.3.

The defensive midfielder Sahin (18) moves into a safety player's position and the other defensive midfielder Bender (6) moves into a balanced position in the centre.

Red No.3 wins the ball and passes to No.11. Sahin (18) moves to put pressure on the ball immediately.

Sokratis (25) and Mkhitaryan (10) mark the potential receivers of the ball (red No.10 and No.6).

There is compactness and a numerical superiority created at the back (3 v 2).

Option 3

The winger Blaszczykowski (16) is the man in possession and the full back Piszczek (26) makes an overlapping run.

The defensive midfielder Bender (6) is the safety player.

Tactical Situation 3

The ball is directed to the right winger Blaszczykowski (16) who drops back to receive and the full back Piszczek (26) makes an overlapping run.

The defensive midfielder Bender (6) shifts into a safety player's position.

The red centre back No.5 wins the ball from Blaszczykowski and passes to No.6. Bender (6) puts pressure on him and Mkhitaryan (10) moves to double mark him.

Piszczek (26) drops back immediately and Sahin (18) marks red No.10 closely.

This diagram shows another option in the same situation. Red No.5 wins the ball and passes to No.11. The new man in possession has plenty of space in front of him before the defensive midfielder Bender (6) is able to close him down.

As there is an open ball situation, the red forwards move forward and the Borussia Dortmund defenders drop back to prevent a pass in behind the defensive line.

The aim of Bender (6) is to close down red No.11 without going to ground, in order to give time to Piszczek (26) to drop into an effective defensive position.

Mkhitaryan (10) drops back and provides balance in midfield.

Tactical Analysis: Both Defensive Midfielders Are Safety Players

Option 1

The ball is in the No.10's (Mkhitaryan) possession and both the defensive midfielders are safety players.

Tactical Situation 1

The ball is directed to Mkhitaryan (the No.10) this time. The red centre back No.5 moves to put pressure on him.

Both Borussia Dortmund defensive midfielders are in safety player positions.

Red No.3 wins the ball and passes to No.8. Bender (6) puts pressure on the ball together with Sahin (18) immediately, while Reus (11) shifts inside to help triple mark red No.8.

Blaszczykowski (16) marks No.6 who is a potential receiver and Sokratis (25) marks No.10 closely who moves towards a potential passing lane. The path to red No.9 is blocked by Bender (6) so he is not marked closely. Hummels (15) provides cover for Sokratis.

Option 2

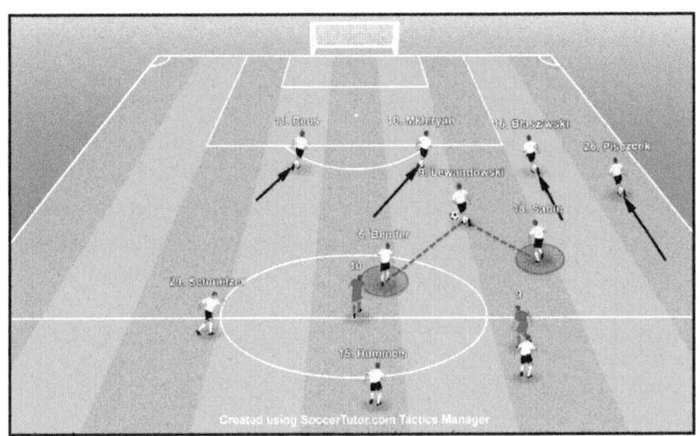

On this occasion the ball has been passed to the centre forward (9) who has dropped back.

Borussia' Dortmund's No.9 turns and the other forwards make movements to receive. Both defensive midfielders are the safety players.

Tactical Situation 2

The ball is directed to the centre forward Lewandowski (9) who drops back to receive unmarked.

Lewandowski tries to turn and pass to the forward moving attacking midfielders. Red No.5 contests him, wins the ball and passes to No.6. Sahin (18) puts pressure on No.6 immediately and Bender (6) shifts into a covering position.

The Borussia Dortmund right back Piszczek (26) makes a recovery run as quickly as possible and Sokratis (25) marks red No.10.

Tactical Analysis: The Winger Is The Safety Player

Option

The right back Piszczek (26) has the ball in an advanced position near the sideline and the right winger Blaszczykowski (16) is in a deeper position (safety player).

Tactical Situation

The ball is directed to the forward moving full back Piszczek (26). Piszczek and Blaszczykowski (16) make synchronised movements. Blaszczykowski drops back at the right moment and becomes the safety player.

Red No.3 wins the ball and passes to No.11. Blaszczykowski (16) moves to immediately close the new man in possession down.

Sahin (18) marks red No.10 closely. Bender (6) moves into a covering position for Blaszczykowski.

Tactical Analysis: The Def. Midfielder And The Winger Are The Safety Players

Option 1

Mkhitaryan (the No.10) has the ball. The defensive midfielder Bender (6) and the right winger Blaszczykowski (16) are the safety players.

As the right full back Piszczek (26) has moved forward, Blaszczykowski cannot also be in an advanced position.

Tactical Situation 1

The ball is directed to Mkhitaryan (10) who is positioned between the opposition's midfield and defensive lines.

The right back Piszczek (26) makes an overlapping run and the winger Blaszczykowski drops back.

Blaszczykowski and the defensive midfielder Bender (6) are the safety players.

As soon as Mkhitaryan (10) loses possession to red No.4, the defensive midfielder Bender (6) moves to close him down. At the same time the two Dortmund wingers Blaszczykowski (16) and Reus (11) move inside and close to the ball area either to help mark the potential receivers (red No.6 and No.8).

Sahin (18) moves forward to mark red No.10 closely and Piszczek (26) drops back immediately.

Option 2

The centre forward Lewandowski (9) has dropped back and received the ball. The other two forwards (No.10 and No.11) make movements to receive in advanced positions.

The winger (16) and the defensive midfielder (6) are the safety players.

Tactical Situation 2

The ball is directed to the centre forward Lewandowski (9) who drops back to receive unmarked and the full back Piszczek (26) makes an overlapping run. The right winger Blaszczykowski (16) drops back.

Blaszczykowski and the defensive midfielder Bender (6) are the safety players.

Red No.5 wins possession from Lewandowski (9) and passes to No.6. Blaszczykowski (16) moves to close him down immediately. At the same time, the defensive midfielder Bender (6) moves into a supporting position and Piszczek (26) drops back.

Sahin (18) marks red No.10 closely and there is a superiority in numbers at the back and compactness in the defensive line.

Session For This Tactical Situation *(3 Practices)*

1. Retaining Safety Players when Building Up Play in a Dynamic 4 Zone 9 v 10 Transition Game

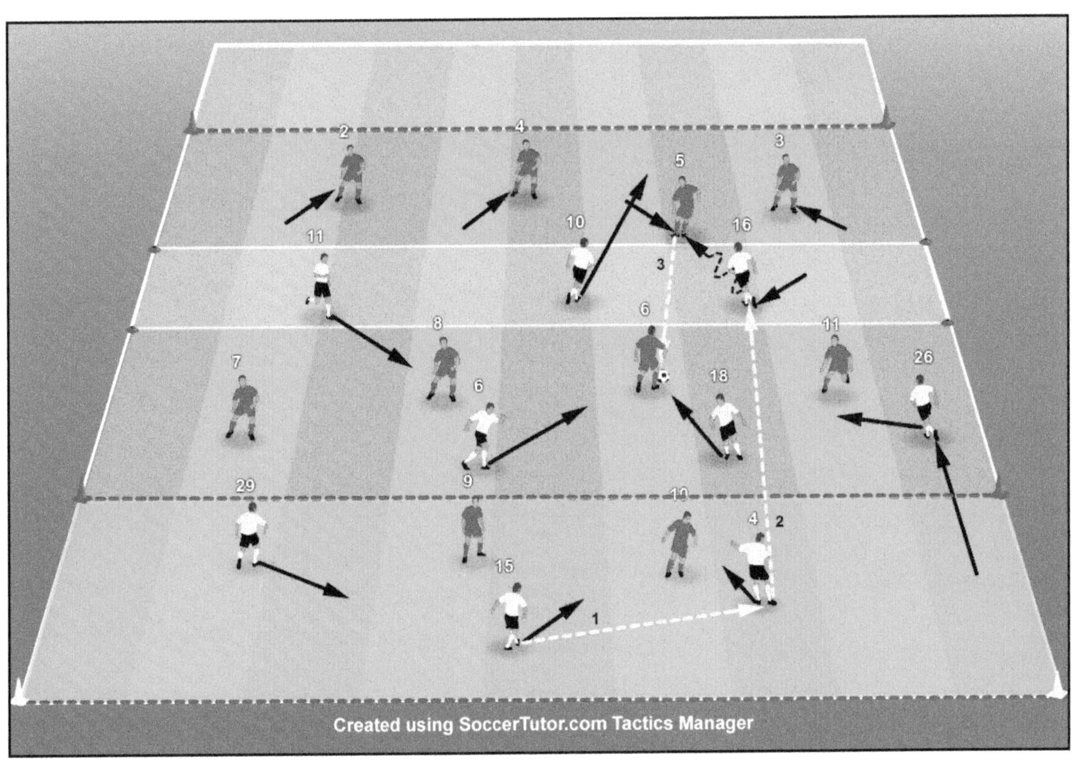

Objective

The players work on retaining at least one safety player when building up play.

Description

We play a 9 v 10 transition game in a 45 x 65 yard area. In the first low zone (45 x 25 yards) we have 4 yellow defenders and 2 red forwards. The 2 yellow defensive midfielders and the 4 red midfielders are positioned in the second zone (45 x 20 yards). The 3 yellow attacking midfielders are in the third white zone (45 x 5 yards) and the 4 red defenders are in the fourth zone (45 x 15 yards).

The yellow defenders aim to retain a numerical advantage in the low zone, make a forward pass towards the 3 midfielders and then score by receiving a pass within the third white zone (the offside rule is applied) or by dribbling the ball through the red end line. The full back on the strong side moves forward during the attack and a 3 v 2 advantage in the low zone remains.

If the yellows lose possession, they try to prevent the reds from dribbling the ball through the middle red line or the red end red line. The yellows aim to regain possession within 6 seconds. The reds can also achieve both aims (dribbling the ball through the middle and the red end line).

Restrictions

1. The red forwards and midfielders do not try to block the forward passes towards the yellow attacking midfielders in the third white zone.
2. The red defenders can apply pressure as soon as the forward pass is made. After this there are no restrictions in regards to the zones, except for the red forwards who are not allowed to move out of the low zone.

PROGRESSION

2. Retaining Safety Players when Building Up Play in an 11 v 11 Dynamic 4 Zone Transition Game

Description

This is a progression of the previous practice and is played in 2/3 of a full sized pitch. The yellow players try to pass the ball to the yellow midfielders inside the white zone and they then to score against the goalkeeper in the full sized goal.

If the yellows lose possession, they then try to prevent the reds from dribbling the ball through the red line. Secondly, if a successful pass towards the red forwards in the low zone is achieved, the yellows must try to stop them from scoring in the mini goals.

The yellows aim to regain possession within 6 seconds. The reds can achieve both aims (dribbling the ball through the red line or scoring in the mini goals).

Coaching Points

1. The yellow players need quick reactions after losing possession.
2. Players need to read the specific tactical situation and have accurate passing throughout the practice.
3. There needs to be good synchronisation in the players' movements.

PROGRESSION

3. Retaining Safety Players when Building Up Play in an 11 v 11 Dynamic 4 Zone Transition Game (2)

Created using SoccerTutor.com Tactics Manager

Description

This is a progression of the previous practice with the same aims and restrictions.

The only difference is that the red forwards now try to score against the goalkeeper in a full sized goal.

Lightning Source UK Ltd.
Milton Keynes UK
UKOW07f1833151117
312786UK00003B/71/P

9 781910 491034